BEYOND TOKENISM

Embrace a Sense of Belonging and Stand Out as an Inclusive Leader

CECILIA NTOMBIZODWA MZVONDIWA

10-10-10
Publishing

Publisher
10-10-10 Publishing
Markham, ON Canada

Printed in Canada and the United States of America

To my father:
On June 20, 2022, you transitioned to another life.
Rest In power, Gushungo!
You were my first leader, coach, and mentor.
Specifically, you taught me what true inclusion is.
You cherished the uniqueness in everyone, young or old,
rich or poor, healthy or sick, and you had a way of
making each person feel visible and unique.
Thank you! Here is my daily prayer for you:

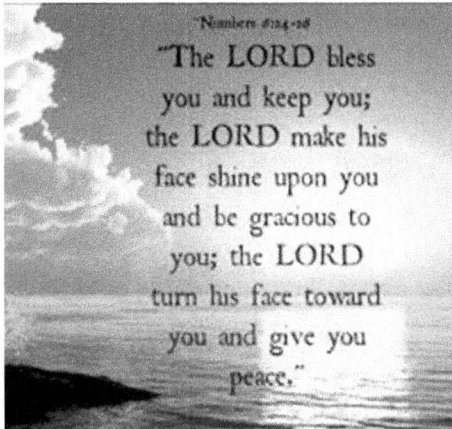

"Numbers 6:24-26

"The LORD bless
you and keep you;
the LORD make his
face shine upon you
and be gracious to
you; the LORD
turn his face toward
you and give you
peace."

TABLE OF CONTENTS

TESTIMONIALS

Cecilia is a deep and thoughtful leader who lives and leads from a place of authentic presence, purpose and self-insight. She brings a powerful perspective to her world's work in the areas of diversity, equity and inclusion. I observe her commitment, diligence and passion for this work, and I value the lens Cecilia views the world through.

Given her background, education and lived experience, she brings a richness to the conversation of inclusive leadership and developing positive workplace cultures. Cecilia weaves into her conversations a strong stance around anti-racism. She is a humanist, mother, teacher, guide and coach.

What Cecilia brings is a willingness to challenge the status quo, catalyze uncomfortable conversations, and a deep desire to make the world a better place for all. I hold immense respect and admiration for Cecilia as a person and what she has accomplished as a leader. What I know for sure is the words captured in this book are words of wisdom and reflect an understanding of the human condition.

As leaders, we are being called to wake up and witness our own humanity, our impact on others, and to consciously create workplace cultures that cultivate a deep sense of belonging for individuals representing all dimensions of diversity. Cecilia is a model of this style of leadership. She is a gift to this world, a champion of human rights and a wisdom holder.

With deep love and respect,

Kristan R. Nielson
Director, Talent Development and Learning (TDL)
JUST CULTURE | HEALTHY TOGETHER | AHS CARES
Alberta Health Services, Calgary Area
www.albertahealthservices.ca
Compassion | Accountability | Respect | Excellence | Safety

* * *

I regard Cecilia Muzvondiwa as both a friend, sister, and colleague. Her story and journey of going from a background of very little resource to the highly successful and impactful person she has developed into, is an inspiration. Having worked on workplace and societal diversity, equity, and inclusion (DE&I) projects with Cecilia, I know firsthand not only of her passion for social justice but also her strategic mind in guiding teams and organizations to meaningful outcomes from DE&I agendas.

Knowing that Cecilia is writing a book fills me with great excitement because the world will get to benefit from her wise insights and generous and thoughtful guidance. At a time when the world is in a state of flux, and countries and communities are backsliding on some of the hard-fought strides of human dignity, justice and fairness, her book carries immense value, and I cannot wait to delve into what she will share with us, to challenge us while also guiding us to better understanding in the way that only she can.

A great asset that Cecilia brings is being exposed to different cultures and the global terrain as a DE&I specialist, which is an important quality in a world that has become increasingly borderless, particularly in the wake of COVID-19. I am both thrilled and honoured to recommend this book by my dear friend, sister, and colleague, and believe the world will be a better place because this book has been written.

Dumi Senda
Founder and CEO | Dumi Senda Ltd
7 Lennon Drive | Crownhill | Milton Keynes | MK8 0AR
Tel: +44 (0) 79 3282 3902
Email: CoachDumi@dumisenda.com
Web: www.dumisenda.com

* * *

Cecilia expresses herself in a deep, authentic way that forges solid connections with all people regardless of status or background. She creates harmony, collaboration, and mutual understanding, both in her personal and professional engagements. She has found a way to simplify complex human issues and ideas through her flawless prompt decision making process and communication. I continue to be impressed by her powerful communication that is gentle yet inspiring. Cecilia has been championing diversity, equity, and inclusion for as long as I have known her. She has a unique touch in creating excitement and imparting wisdom to both junior and senior professionals. She empowers individuals to make best choices, which leads to greater connections, collaboration, impact, and success. I recommend this book as it is coming from a heart-centered space. We are all leaders and can benefit from creating safe spaces that provide a sense of belonging to all those around us.

Blessed Daka MBA. CTP. CPA.
Banking Finance Executive
Co-founder of Friend Foundation of Zimbabwe
Business and Risk Programs @ Wells Fargo
11625 N Community Rd, Charlotte, NC
MAC D1185-060 I Office (980) 260-7498 I Mobile (704) 516-5526

* * *

Thank you, Cecilia, for speaking to the unspoken truths about inclusion. To be truly non-tokenistic and increase diversity in an organization, leaders must focus on creating a sense of belonging for all.

From our first encounter working to make change in our organization, I saw your commitment to leading through love and acceptance as opposed to instilling fear and guilt. You speak to and guide leaders through self-reflection and acceptance, to step into the uncomfortable spaces and do the work to make those spaces safe. I have no doubt that this book will be a resource for others who wish to move beyond performative inclusion.

Karen Chinaleong-Brooks BSc, MPH,
Senior Patient Engagement Consultant
Inaugural Chair Diversity and Racial Equity (DaRE)
Workforce Resource Group, AHS

ACKNOWLEDGEMENTS

I would like to thank **Raymond Aaron** for helping me write and publish this book. Raymond, you amaze me; you have been blessed and you have shared that blessing with many. I want to thank my book architect Barbara Powers. Every Wednesday, you called me to nudge me, and it worked! Lisa, thank you for your work on editing this book! Thank you, Mike, Jody, and Liz, for your work in the background.

To My Family
I would like to thank my daughter, Mia Isabella Mzvondiwa, for the inspiration. Every day, I think of what legacy I leave for Mia, and writing this book is part of my legacy for her.

My Team at Global People First!
You shared in my vision of a more inclusive world for us and for our children. Thank you so much for all you do in your corner of the world; together we have moved the dial toward a more equitable and inclusive society. **Blessed Muzondiwa**-Daka, you are a sister and a friend; thank you for being my sounding board and light of hope. **Dumi Senda**, you are my little brother turned big brother; your vision and focus on the space of diversity, equity and inclusion inspire me. **Bigson Gumbeze**, we have come a long way, friend, from helping people on the streets of Zimbabwe to fighting bullying in New Zealand; we have

always shared similar visions of adding value to society. **Karen kchinaleong-Brooks**, you are a rock, authentic and articulate in the space of diversity and inclusion. Thank you for all the contributions you make.

John Maxwell: Founder of the John Maxwell Team

I want to thank John for his leading by example. John is a man of faith and a guru in leadership. I have learnt a lot from him and his team, which includes **Paul Martinelli**. You taught me to remove self-limiting beliefs. **Chris Robinson**, you always said to trust the process, and it works. **Roddy Galbraith,** you taught me how to rock the stage, the keynote speaker since have been your training. **And Christian Simpson**, you are one of my favourite coaches of all time! You all contributed to my development and certification as a speaker, coach, and trainer. Thank you.

To Tyler Shandro, Minister of Justice and Solicitor General, Government of Alberta

Since my appointment as a hate crimes community liaison, I have been inspired by your determination to tackle hate and all forms of discrimination.

To the JSG community engagement team that is supporting us in the work that we do to prevent, manage, and repair harm caused by hate, thank you. Thank you, **Jessica Thompson (Solgen), Montana Kokoski, Patricia Rzechowka, Barret Weber, Kesia Muthuthotatil** and **Sarah Gastard. Thank you to my colleague Landon Turlock for sharing your passion and knowledge in hate crimes.**

Sage Lavine, Founder of Women Rocking Business

Sage, it was in January 2020, through the Facebook challenge, that you and your team offered me the invaluable gift of the yearlong Entrepreneurial Leadership Academy. The training was a moment of transformation for me. I thank your coaching team: **Shannon Fisher, Theresa Kepple, Clare Cui, Sirena Andrea, Shana James, Meghan Neeley and Reverend Deborah Johnson.** You ladies helped me find myself and taught me so much; you will always be close to my heart as you kept me sane and developing as a businesswoman during the most challenging time of COVID-19.

Deborah Smart and the Learning and Employee Development Department at AHS

Deb, you have shown me that true leadership is about vulnerability and courage. Since I joined your team, you and the team members welcomed me and made me feel accepted for who I am. Everyone individually reached out and offered to help me feel welcome. Thank you, **Alicia Holm, Julie Warner, Andrea Matovitch, Nina Redding, Christina Heinrich, Stephanie Van Den Biggelaar, Lisa Arlint, Lisa Zederayko, Robbin Sutherland, Pamela Menard, Shalini Mathias** and **Laurene Booker.** Thank you to my director, Kristan Nielson, who taught me how to slow down and be aware of the human experience.

Todd Gilchrest, former VP of People, Legal and Privacy at Alberta Health Services

When George Floyd was murdered on May 25, 2020, the murder sparked a series of civil rights demonstrations globally. Organizations were putting out statements condemning racism. I reached out to

For bonuses go to ...

Todd as my VP to discuss our position as an organization and how I was impacted as a black person. I was really inspired by how Todd created safety for the conversation, was vulnerable in accepting that he was open to learning, could make mistakes and was there to listen. Todd, you taught me that outstanding leadership is the ability to lean into discomfort, vulnerability, and the willingness to listen.

Marni Panas, Manager of Diversity, and Inclusion at Alberta Health Services
I met Marni close to six years ago when she was championing diversity and inclusion. She came to visit Grande Prairie, and I listened to her presentation. I was challenged to understand the LBGTQ community and understand her as a transgender woman. I have developed a friendship with Marni throughout the years and she has been both an ally and cheerleader for me. Marni inspired me to share my story and to believe in working toward a more accepting and inclusive world.

Katherine Todd
I met Katherine when she was the sponsor for the anti-racism committee for Alberta Health Services. I reached out to Katherine to understand how she would support the committee as a Caucasian woman. I have since been inspired by her leadership. She is an active ally and is supportive of creating a more inclusive environment. Thank you, Katherine, for your leadership and championing diversity, equity, and inclusion in our organization.

Dobko and Wheaton Law Firm
I thank the lawyers—**Gerry Dobko, Mike Wheaton, Lihn Wisekal, Joseph Canavan and Allan Wale**—for allowing me to learn how to

practice law in Alberta. I thank all the ladies at the law firm: **Kelly Blake, Debra L., Gloria Gilles, Terri Dickson, Nancy V., Kelly E. and the late Shirley.**

Community Foundation Board of Northwest
I am grateful for the encouragement and support from my board colleagues: Todd Russel, Lydia Sadiq, Eunice Friesen, Travis Jensen, Ralph Wohlgemuth, Simon Bossen, Donna Kock, Andrew Boylan, Todd Tremblay, Natasha Collins-Decoster, Stephen Hinckley, Helen Amy Richards and the staff of Laura LaValley, Rhonda Reichet, Shelley Younger, Brittany Kelsely and Devon Potter.

To my friends who saw the potential in me and believed in me:
Patrick Daka, Prabjot Maholtra, Philip Omunga, Paul Blasetti, Jodi Manz-Henezi, Judy John, Noah Nemhara, Janet Gwena, Cindy Yaceyko, Claudette Lachance, Neilum, Lena Benston, Chaka Rukobo, Patience Farai Madambi, Dr. Michael Onyebuchi Eze, Ignatius Makumborenga, Leopold Boroma, Winnie Mhaka, Nathaniel Madzivanyika, Rachel Nyirasengimana, Dunsi Strohschein, Stella Jonah, Patricia Nhongo, Nomsa Maromo, Silindile Ncube, Leticia Ngwenya, Nqo Jackie Ndlovu, Modester Maganga, Susan Wildon, Alice Maradha,Tabeth Kausi, Grace Vembo, Nontando Vuma and Majuta Trust.

263 True North ladies
I want to extend my gratitude to the Zimbabwean women living in Canada. These women have been supportive of my journey and work, and they provide content that is aimed at empowering women. Ladies, I don't want to mention only a few, but thank you all for the things you do that have inspired me and pushed me to get out of my comfort

zone and do the things I am passionate about. Thank you to Sharon Njobo who is the Firestarter of the group

Thank you to the following priests and sisters who had a hand in shaping my life as a young adult. You offered me guidance and planted the seeds of faith, integrity, and leadership in my life. Special thanks to the Dominican Missionary sisters who were my teachers and mentors.

- Sr. Prisca Zhakata OP
- Sister Bernadette Helegwa OP
- Sr. Tendai Makonese OP
- Sr. Ferreira Wenzel OP
- Sr. Gundula Haufele OP
- Father Valerian Shirima SJ
- Father Brian Enright SJ
- Father Silvester Igboanyika
- Father Michael Kyalo SJ
- Father Odomaro Mubanjizi SJ
- Father Lawrence Daka SJ

FOREWORD

Beyond Tokenism: How to Embrace a Sense of Belonging and Stand Out as an Inclusive Leader is a just-in-time tool that you need now more than ever. You are living in a much-polarized world, and you no doubt see an increase in misinformation, disinformation, and fear that fuels extremism and hate. In addition, you have been challenged by the covid-19 pandemic, inflation, and a looming recession.

To heal and move on as a member of the human race, you must celebrate diversity, focus on inclusion, and create a sense of belonging in your community and your workplace. This book is intended to give you the knowledge and tools you need to be an inclusive leader. Cecilia Mzvondiwa provides tools for you to identify and mitigate your own biases and develop psychologically safe spaces that in turn create a sense of belonging and inclusion. This book is an excellent resource if you have struggled with discomfort and fear of saying the wrong things, or simply not knowing where to start.

Beyond Tokenism contributes new vocabulary in the diversity, equity, and inclusion space. Cecilia writes from a heart-centered space. She invites you to lean into the discomfort, and creates a safe space for you to engage and see yourself without dwelling on guilt and shame. A skillful storyteller, Cecilia weaves facts and challenges assumptions while including her own story within the broader story of humanity.

So many people are prisoners of prejudice, ignorance, and bias. In other words, we are all victims of some sort. If you want to understand more about humans, the human brain, and the human heart in the space of diversity, equity, and inclusion, read this book.

Raymond Aaron
New York Times **Bestselling Author**

CHAPTER ONE

The 2020 Global Reset

"Change is the law of life. And those who look only to the past or present are certain to miss the future."
– John F. Kennedy

Coronavirus, aka COVID-19 Pandemic

When news started to circulate, in December 2019, about a virus in Wuhan, China, our global world had no idea what was unfolding. We all continued to plan life as usual. I, for one, planned a trip to Zimbabwe. I live in Canada, and I was born in Zimbabwe. My parents are advanced in age, so it has been my practice for 12 years to go home every year and spend a month with them. Usually, I would make this trip in December, but this time I had just come back to work in September from maternity leave. I booked to travel on February 14, 2020, on Valentine's Day. As the news about the virus spread in Wuhan, and lockdown was initiated in Wuhan, it seemed like the virus was under control and a problem for China. I had forgotten that we now live in a global village where we are mutually interconnected and share our mutual vulnerability. I was booked to be back in Canada on March 10, and then to proceed to

California on March 13, 2020, for a business conference. After that, I was booked as a keynote speaker at a conference in New Zealand, in August 2020.

The rest of my plans are history. We landed back in Canada on March 10, 2020, and the World Health Organization declared the coronavirus a pandemic on March 11, 2020; and on March 14, 2020, Canadian borders were closed. I dodged the bullet! The world was shut down in March 2020. It seemed as if someone had pressed a pause button on planet Earth. There was such disruption: the magnitude of change overnight, fear, economies at a standstill, geopolitics confusion, and humans confined to homes. The supply chain of goods was disrupted. A new vocabulary emerged: expressions such as social and physical distancing, remote work, essential workers, essential travel, and quarantine. I had spent 13 years working in health care. I had associated protective equipment like masks, gloves and gowns with our nurses and doctors; outside that, it was Michael Jackson, whom I last saw wearing a mask outside the hospital setting. Masks and sanitizers became the norm.

For as long as I can remember, I have not seen streets empty, planes grounded, or cars parked. I am a frequent flyer and have travelled extensively. March 10 was the last time I flew in 2020. You might think that it is a luxury, not a necessity, but to me, it was a dramatic change in life. As the year progressed and numbers went up, the news covered nothing but the virus; humanity was challenged. An unprecedented, unplanned transformation was set in motion for both the inhabitants of the planet Earth and the climate of the planet. Mass graves in China, Italy, Spain, and other countries scared the wits out of me. The saddest of all this was that the people died alone without families. They were buried by strangers. As a human race, we have grappled with understanding deep questions about life; philosophers and religions have postulated answers to life and death questions, and we are still at a loss when it comes to the meaning of life and what happens after we die. Now for people to die in such numbers and in this way, confirmed the fragility and flimsiness of human life. There was talk about past pandemics, like the Spanish flu, HIV, AIDS, SARS, and Ebola. However, there has been nothing like COVID-19 in our lifetime!

In 2020, the civil rights movement, sparked by the murder of George Floyd, by the Minneapolis police on May 25, showed that racism is rife—not just in America but in our global world. There is racism and hate against people of colour; an indiscriminate negative perception or emotion toward people of black-African descent, rooted in colonization and slavery, and expressed as an exaggerated fear, hatred and hostility toward black people or black communities. Anti-black racism is perpetuated by negative stereotypes and social structures that discriminate, marginalize, and exclude the black population from social, political, and civic life.

In 2021, as the pandemic waves continued, hate crimes rose. In Canada, police-reported hate crimes increased by 37% to 3,360 incidents in 2021. Compared with 2019, hate crimes have increased by 72% over the last two years. More hate crimes targeting religion (+67%) (including Jewish, Muslim, and Catholic) and sexual orientation (+64%) accounted for most of the national change, along with more incidents targeting race or ethnicity (+6%). In addition, the COVID-19 pandemic further exposed and exacerbated issues related to discrimination, including hate crimes. For example, according to data from the 2020 General Social Survey on Social Identity, racialized groups were more than twice as likely to report having experienced discrimination, since the start of the pandemic, compared with the rest of the population.

Humanity is reckoning with the ugly past and the dark present. Starting in the 19th century, Canada was home to a system of residential schools, operated mainly by churches, that Indigenous children were forced to attend. The system declined during the 1970s, with the last school closing in 1996. For decades, most Indigenous children in Canada were taken from their families and forced into boarding schools. Many never returned home, and their families were given only vague explanations or none. In June 2021, an Indigenous community in British Columbia said it had found evidence of what happened to some of its missing children: a mass grave containing the remains of 215 children on the grounds of a former residential school.

There was outrage about this colonial practice, and as I write, a few steps have been taken to respond to this egregious act. A delegation of Indigenous people from Canada visited the Pope in Rome, in the spring of 2022, among them some residential school survivors who shared their stories. In July of 2022, the head of the Catholic Church, Pope Francis, made what he called a pilgrimage of penance. He visited some communities in Canada and apologized for the role of the Catholic Church in residential schools. There has been much debate in the media and among Indigenous people about the apology, some calling it a "missed opportunity."

Systemic inequalities exposed by the COVID-19 pandemic and fueled by the intensified civil rights movement, have awakened our collective consciousness on diversity, equity, and inclusion. The coronavirus humanized us. The pandemic highlighted the inequalities that minority groups face. For example, BBC, in their coverage of "Why is COVID-19 killing people of colour in the U.K.?" had this staggering data to share: 44% of the doctors in NHS are people of colour, and of all the doctors who died of the virus, 95% were doctors of colour. The data is a sad revelation of the realities of what racism is doing silently every day in our communities.

A report by the Public Health Agency of Canada on the impact of COVID-19 provides that the effect has been worse for some groups, including racialized communities. Although race-based data are not consistently available across Canada, local sources indicate that racialized communities are disproportionately impacted by COVID-19. These disproportionate impacts among racialized and Indigenous communities are not due to biological differences between groups or populations. Instead, they reflect existing health inequities strongly influenced by specific social and economic determinants, such as income, education, employment, and housing. I could go on with examples in other countries, but you get the idea of the magnitude of the issues around our human race.

Members of racialized communities were found to be more likely to experience inequitable living and working conditions that make them more susceptible to COVID-19, such as lower incomes, precarious employment, overcrowded housing and limited access to health and social services. For example, many care providers in long-term care facilities in Canada, the United Kingdom, and the United States, are racialized women. Racialized employees also comprise a significant component of Canadian agriculture and food production systems. The working conditions in these facilities, higher risk living conditions at home, and the use of public transport are all factors that put these employees at an increased risk for COVID-19. The global response to the killing of George Floyd in Minneapolis is an indicator that, as humans, we are not okay when our fellow humans are treated inhumanely. There were mass demonstrations around the world. Despite the fear of the COVID-19 virus, people took the risk to show their disgust and voice that racism is not okay. In the demonstrations, there were people of all shades, ages, sex, and shapes, sending a strong message that gone are the days when it was okay to strip a fellow human being of their dignity and intrinsic rights.

As many jobs moved from office space to kitchen tables, bedrooms and living rooms, a new way of working was being baked and birthed simultaneously. New fashion trends emerged: growing a beard and wearing a suit jacket and shirt with pyjama pants. While organizations whose work could be done remotely were relieved that at least business continued and, in some ways, better productivity was realized, there was a divide between the employees who had the privilege to work from home, and those that had no choice but to be onsite as their jobs could not be done remotely. For example, doctors, nurses, and healthcare frontline staff stayed onsite. Human resources departments were challenged by the choice of some workers who felt it was their right to stay home or quit their jobs to protect themselves from the virus. There was much debate in the summer of 2021 when, after the vaccine was deployed, there was a sense of hope that things could return to "normal," and people could return to the office. New buzzwords like "the great resignation" emerged.

The excitement and hope quickly dissipated as different variants continued to challenge us. First, it was Delta, then Omicron, and who knows what the next one will be. The discussion changed from returning to work or to the office, to making permanent choices about working remotely or choosing a hybrid approach. Some managers and leaders experienced a loss of control and fear of managing remote teams. Employees experienced a sense of autonomy and flexibility. The ability to work without a commute, work in comfortable clothes and not worry about office politics is appealing to many.

The pool of candidates for recruiters expanded. No longer confined to geographic locations, it was great to attract the best candidates, and most job postings now indicate if this is remote work. Only some things were going on well for everyone. There were and are still issues around equitable access to space working from home. There are some hardware and software and connection issues for some. Some people had no Wi-Fi or good bandwidth in their homes. Others had more family members and children logging in for school from home. Homeschooling became a significant challenge for parents.

The global pandemic threw a wrench into business operations of all sizes. The emergence of remote work challenged the traditional work mentality. Managers struggled with how they exercised control over staff who were working remotely. In addition, the emergence of digital forms of communication caused mental health issues for many workers.

As the public eye fixated on racial injustice in the U.S. last year, organizations sensed a new level of urgency in addressing diversity, equity, and inclusion—or DEI—in the workplace. Yet, despite many bold statements, and commitments, there needs to be more compelling evidence that we are closer to a more inclusive global world. Most underrepresented groups remain on the periphery of society. Most organizations have been influenced by "comply or explain" policies and regulations. Some counties and organizations have shifted from "soft targets" to "hard quotas." This unfolding situation is an opportunity to take transformative action against systemic racism and discrimination. Diverse leadership has a positive impact on workforce initiatives. Leaders search for proven practices to promote diversity and inclusion.

As the coronavirus pandemic slowed global commerce to a crawl in early 2020, emissions of nitrogen oxides (NOx)—which create ozone, a danger to human health and to the climate—decreased 15% globally, with local reductions as high as 50%, according to a study led by scientists at NASA's Jet Propulsion Laboratory in Southern California. As a result of the lower NOx emissions, by June 2020, global ozone levels had dropped to a level that policymakers thought would take at least 15 years to reach by conventional means, such as regulations. Global climate change noted a 5.4% reduction in carbon dioxide emissions in 2020.

COVID-19 has changed the world. The pandemic has caused devastation, pain and loss, with no corner of the globe untouched. But for some scientists, the unprecedented disruption has also brought about a previously unimaginable opportunity. The dramatic fall in air pollution that accompanied countries going into lockdown has provided a unique natural experiment, enabling scientists to probe some of the long-standing mysteries surrounding cloud formation. In doing so, they have better understood the complicated interactions between air pollution, weather, and climate.

Social distancing-induced remote working for white-collar jobs may trigger longer-term changes in business travel practices.

Reduced industrial and transport activity will improve local air quality, potentially easing pollution-related respiratory illness.

Climate-focused social movements will have to adapt to new forms of organization without traditional mass protests.

Mental Health – Trauma and Moral Distress Issues

We have all experienced one or more mental health symptoms, from stress, anxiety, depression and trauma to loss and grief. A lot of data and information shows the impact on different generations. Young people missed their exams, or graduation and prom, something that they had looked forward to in their lives. There were the effects of isolation, being stuck at home and not being able to play with friends. Attending school online gave them no break from gadgets like iPads, phones, and computers.

I have coached clients who have struggled because their roles have changed overnight, and they need their job to pay the bills. In my legal practice, parents have struggled with fundamental moral beliefs, those who want their children vaccinated and those against vaccines. Some families have not come together since the onset of COVID-19, due to arguments stemming from differences in fundamental beliefs. In addition, there has been a surge in domestic violence. Before COVID-19, close to 50% of all marriages ended in divorce. Some of the shaky marriages and relationships were saved by the fact that couples and partners worked away from home, and they saw each other for a short time. However, being locked down revealed the difficulties and differences that couples had. Those differences and issues were amplified, and mental health issues emerged as there were no outlets. Throughout the pandemic, anxiety, depression, sleep disruptions and thoughts of suicide have increased for many young adults. They have also experienced several pandemic-related consequences, such as closures of universities, transitioning to remote work, and loss of income or employment, which may contribute to poor mental health.

As a result, more ideation of suicide was found in this group. Throughout the pandemic, many people across the globe have experienced job or income loss, which has generally affected their mental health. Adults experiencing household job loss during the pandemic have consistently reported higher rates of symptoms of anxiety and/or depressive disorder compared to adults not experiencing household job loss. In many third-world countries, unemployment is high; most survive on daily activities like buying and selling. Lockdowns meant no food on the table for some families.

To help slow the spread of coronavirus, many schools and childcare centre worldwide have closed, and some transitioned to virtual instruction for at least some time. With these closures, children and their parents are experiencing ongoing disruption and changes to their daily routines. Research during the pandemic highlights concerns about poor mental health and well-being for children and their parents. Parents were juggling their jobs while helping children log into classes and stay focused, and all the stress resulted in significant health pressure on parents. Both parents and their children have experienced worsening mental health since the start of the pandemic, and women with children are more likely than their male counterparts to report deteriorating mental health.

Essential workers during the COVID-19 pandemic, such as healthcare providers, grocery store employees and mail and package delivery personnel, have shown high rates of poor mental health outcomes. In addition, these workers are generally required to work outside their homes and may be unable to practice social distancing. Consequently, they are at increased risk of contracting coronavirus and exposing other household members.

As I write the final chapters of this book, in November 2022, COVID-19 is no longer as scary as it was. In some countries, the vaccine is now available for children under five. As a result, most countries are transitioning from a pandemic to an endemic as many people gain immunity from vaccination and natural infection; there is less transmission and a decline in COVID-19 hospitalization and death. As the virus slows down, new threats to human security continue to emerge, and there is a growing concern about the spread of monkeypox. Although the disease has been detected in some demographics, like the gay population, the threat reminds us that we cannot be complacent. Our shared humanity is challenged by many dangers, including climate change, wars, and recessions, and in all this, leadership is critical, and inclusive leadership is a must.

I started writing this book in the summer of 2021 and had planned to finish it and have it published by August 2022. As happens with life, we make plans, and life happens. My father's health started to go downhill in October 2021. I wanted to go and see him; travel restrictions were still in place. I waited until January 2022 and realized that I needed to go and spend quality time with him while he was still up and about and able to visit with us. I travelled on February 14, 2022. My daughter and I had to get our PCR tests and meet all the travel restrictions. We spent quality time with my father for 2 weeks and travelled back to Canada. Three months later, my father passed, on June 20, 2022. I was so grateful for the opportunity to spend time with my father and to pay my last respects. My father was a man of the people; we were overwhelmed by the number of people who showed up to pay their respects at the funeral, and by the messages and his legacy of how much he made each person he met feel special. On the day of his burial, we had warm weather. The night after that, we had cold and wind and then rain for a week. June is the middle of winter in Zimbabwe; normally there are no rains. There were close to a thousand people at our homestead for the funeral. There was singing and dancing for two days. No one got COVID-19. I am so grateful that my father held on until it was safe for people to gather. At his funeral, I reflected more on the topic of diversity. The people that came, young and old, male, and female, had different religious beliefs and sexual orientations. My father was an inclusive leader for a man of his time and culture.

This topic is close to my heart because it strikes a chord. I am not talking about something I read or know about. It is about my lived experiences and something I feel deeply about. In my life journey, I have been invited to the party many times but never asked to dance, and I lost my confidence. I now came to realize that being requested is not enough. Diversity has failed me. I sat at tables where I was the token of diversity, the only black immigrant woman. Still, I was never indeed invited to be my authentic self and participate fully. In that case, diversity served the organization in pulling out numbers but did not do anything for me. In fact, it failed me. It felt like a sacrificial lamb, having a title without the power, or being a toothless bulldog. I remember that people would not make eye contact with me at the table when I spoke. No matter what ideas I shared, they were not acknowledged. Long story short, that portfolio struggled from lack of innovation; high turnover and engagement went down. I know my boss forgot about how they treated me, but those experiences are still alive in me, just like the famous saying that people will forget what you say and what you know but will never forget how you make them feel. This is a challenge for all leaders. What legacy are you building?

Staff engagement is the number one driver of productivity and innovation; it is a competitive driver. Think about it: 80% of your operating budget is on talent; why waste money on talent if you do not allow people to contribute fully by creating an inclusive environment where people use their discretionary effort to go above and beyond the job description?

There have been very few moments when I could be my authentic self and feel I matter. I have been deprived of the magical moment of a sense of belonging. Belonging is fundamental; as humans, we are compelled genetically to belong. I grew up very aware of my strength and areas of improvement. Unfortunately, my decision to move from Zimbabwe to Canada caused me to lose my strengths. It was when I realized that I still had all my inert talents and skills. All I needed was to feel psychologically safe to unleash all my superpowers.

The NeuroLeadership Institute reports that research shows that diverse teams are better at creative problem solving, error detection and logical problem solving, and have more business success; however, focusing on diversity is only a first step. Without inclusion, we stand to miss out on those benefits. I would like to offer this story as I close this first chapter.

The story is about a church that was going to get a new pastor. The council chair wrote down the list of qualities he wanted in the new pastor, gave it to the bishop and waited for the pastor to show up that resembled his values. Instead, they got a woman minister who was unlike him in many ways. From preaching to conversation style, to the fact that she was a woman, she was the opposite of the council chair. The council chair criticized her every turn and kept looking for the slightest infraction. Finally, he invited her to his boat, moored on the Willamette, and spent more time with her to iron out their differences. She agreed, and they met at the waterfront bridge and set off. After going a few dozen yards from shore, the pastor said she was cold and wanted to get her jacket from her car. The chairperson said, "I can take us back to shore." But the clergywoman said, "Don't bother," and she stepped out of the boat and walked on water back to the shore.

He muttered under his breath as she walked on water away from the chairman. "I can't believe they sent a pastor who can't even swim." What does this story tell you about prejudice and bias? As you ponder this question, you can proceed to the next chapter to interact with more ideas on diversity, equity, and inclusion.

CHAPTER TWO

Diversity, Equity, Inclusion & Belonging

*Diversity is about all of us figuring out
how to walk through this world together."*
– Jacqueline Woodson

Diversity

*"Diversity relates to the extent of demographic identities
within teams, age, disability, ethnicity, gender, race, nationality,
sexual orientation, socioeconomic background,
to mention a few examples."*
– Harvard Business Review

The term "diversity" evokes different emotions in different people. For some, it is that annoying word that evokes discomfort, guilt, blame, excuses, dread and, for some, anger, and frustration. For others, it provides hope that, as humans, we can finally move toward civilization by recognizing humanity, dignity, and intrinsic rights for all. There is a whole spectrum of how people feel, and myriad definitions exist.

While it is most challenging to come up with an agreed definition of a term that is sensitive and important such as diversity, it is also helpful to give a working definition to enable the discussion. First, I will share some of the definitions used in different settings. Then, I will provide my own definition that I am using in this book. It is a simple fact that diversity, as it relates to human beings, is in our DNA. Science has shown us that no two people are alike; simple facts like our fingerprints attest to the uniqueness of everyone. Even identical twins remain unique in different ways. The universe is designed for diversity.

Our very existence as human beings is baked on diversity. If we think of the body parts, they are uniquely designed and function together. The irony is that we have used diversity as a negative concept for economic and political reasons.

On the contrary, diversity should be celebrated, as our whole existence is coined on everything unique and diverse that works together for our well-being. I was born into a family of eight siblings. We all have very different personalities and a few physical similarities, but we have this diversity of perspective, thought, experiences, age, sex, gender, and many invisible and intangible differences. Now, on this planet Earth, all eight billion humans are unique. This leads to the simple fact and conclusion that diversity makes us human. For me, diversity is about people. I will say more about this at the end of this chapter. Now I want to share some definitions that different industries and practitioners have provided.

Diversity makes life and living more beautiful and engaging, as it continues to orient and reorient people on how to effectively manage the differences in people and how to work with them for the common good of society. Furthermore, it holistically enriches societies by broadening the experiences and mindsets of people living in each community, through the cross-pollination of ideas, thereby creating opportunities for increased productivity for individuals, teams, and society.

Diversity in the workplace means that an organization employs a diverse team of people reflective of the society in which it exists and operates. Unfortunately, determining what makes the team diverse is more complex. Diversity incorporates all the elements that make individuals unique from one another. While there are infinite differences in humans, most of us subconsciously define diversity by a few social categories, such as gender, race, age, etc.

Everyone in an organization brings diverse perspectives, work and life experiences, and religious and cultural differences. The power of diversity can only be unleashed, and its benefits are reaped when we recognize these differences and learn to respect and value each individual regardless of their background. In our work at Global People First, we have helped companies realize that they must focus on their people first, for their businesses to succeed. The single most important capital for any business is its people. With the great resignation and acute shortage of employment, now more than ever, we are seeing the shifting of power dynamics. Employees have more bargaining power.

Traditionally, there was a narrow focus where diversity was seen to refer to race and gender. Thankfully, the discourse has broadened to include many other aspects of diversity that can be understood and applied. Diversity is any dimension that can differentiate groups and people from one another. In a nutshell, it is about empowering people by respecting and appreciating what makes them different in terms of age, gender, ethnicity, religion, disability, sexual orientation, education, and national origin. In its simplest form, diversity means being composed of differing elements.

The value that diversity adds to the advancement efforts of any team, society or relationship, is key because it makes up for their individual inadequacies and takes everyone to an unfamiliar territory where they would have to stretch their capacities and leave their comfort zone by learning, unlearning and relearning. Diversity allows these differences to be explored in a safe, positive, and nurturing environment. It means understanding one another by surpassing simple tolerance to ensure people genuinely value their differences. This allows us to embrace and celebrate the rich dimensions of diversity within each individual, and value variety in the community and workforce.

Diversity is defined as the presence of differences within a given setting. It is how people are different yet the same at the individual and group levels. Organizational diversity requires examining the makeup of a group to ensure that multiple perspectives are represented. Dereca Blackmom says diversity is a fact, and inclusion is a practice. Diversity is a mix of differences, and inclusion is getting the mix to work together (Dr. Shirley Davis). Attorney and diversity consultant Verna Myers distinguishes between diversity and inclusion, saying, "Diversity is being invited to the party, and inclusion is being asked to dance. Diversity also doesn't require organizations to "lower the bar" for diverse groups. So, a truly diverse and inclusive environment is valuing everyone's contributions and raising the bar for everyone, and not lowering the bar as some might assume.

Diversity represents the full spectrum of human differences. It often describes demographic differences, such as race, religion, gender, sexual orientation, age, socioeconomic status, or physical disability. However, diversity is much more than the visible differences among people. Many companies choose to recognize a broader definition of diversity that encompasses personal differences such as lifestyles, personality characteristics, family composition, education, or tenure. Academics and professionals emphasize the need to acknowledge that these differences also imply differences in world views, perspectives, opinions, and approaches to decision-making, all of which should be considered under the umbrella of diversity. Definitions of diversity are also influenced by the characteristics of generations in the workforce. Compared with previous generations, millennials are the most demographically diverse in the workforce, with 44.2% categorized as part of a minority race or ethnic group. Generation Z will be even more varied. Diversity in race or gender is more common for these generations; therefore, they tend to think of diversity through a wider lens of combined identities, such as being both a "woman and a minority" or "LGBTQ and a first-generation immigrant." Diversity for millennials and future generations will likely be much more about everyone's unique experiences and opinions versus traditional demographic categories (Gallup).

Finally, diversity is not just a responsibility of an H.R. department or even the CEO of an organization. It's an essential topic from both a top-down and a bottom-up perspective. We need our local teams and managers to take inclusion as seriously as we expect from our leadership. Diversity is about the eight billion people that call our planet Earth home—**8 billion hopes, 8 billion dreams, and 8 billion minds!**

Equity

Equity is not about equality. Equality is about sameness; equity is about fairness. Equality is aspirational, and equity is actionable. It's about fairness, levelling the playing field in the hiring and promoting processes and removing barriers. Systemic inequities exposed by the COVID-19 pandemic, and a renewed and intensified awareness of racial injustice, have contributed to the renewed focus on equity.

Equity has also been defined as the "absence of underlying social advantages or disadvantages of power, control, wealth, privilege or prestige." Systemic means it is formalized, accepted, and enforced in the laws, practices and ways of functioning in society. Take apartheid in South Africa, for example; it was embedded into society's very institutions and organizations, influencing policies and procedures. There was an institutionalized divide between race and ethnicity: buses for whites, buses for blacks and Indians, washrooms for blacks, and restrooms for white people. Streets and places were reserved for whites, requiring a pass for other ethnicities to get into town. The institutionalization makes it difficult to root out systemic practices.

Equity acknowledges and seeks to address systemic inequalities. The perception of being treated unfairly can elicit a reaction like feeling disgusted. However, research shows that not only do we dislike unfairness when it's not to our benefit, but we also dislike it even when it benefits us. The NeuroLeadership Institute defines equity as the "absence of systematic disparities…between groups with different levels of underlying social advantage/disadvantage—that is, wealth, power, or prestige"— for example, systemic racism. Our distaste for unfairness is biological and neurological. We saw people take to the streets when George Floyd was murdered. In the same way, we saw millions demonstrating because of the death of Mahsa Amini, a 22-year-old woman detained by the morality police in Iran for showing too much hair, and who died on September 16, 2022, in a hospital under suspicion of police brutality.

Equity refers to an approach that ensures that everyone has the same opportunities. It recognizes that advantages and barriers exist and, as a result, everyone does not start from the same place. It is a process that begins by acknowledging that unequal starting place and works to correct and address the imbalance. Equity ensures that everyone can grow, contribute, and develop, regardless of their identity. Basically, it is the fair and just treatment of all community members. It requires commitment and deliberate attention to strategic priorities, resources, respect, and civility, with ongoing action and assessment of progress toward achieving specified goals.

How does equity relate to diversity and inclusion? Diversity is about individuals and the differences that make up the individuals, both visible and invisible, different perspectives, socioeconomic backgrounds, ideologies, and cultures, to mention a few. On the other hand, inclusion is about accepting the differences discussed above, acknowledging the uniqueness of each individual and providing a safe space for everyone to be accepted for who they are, and being able to bring their best self to work. Many of us have heard young kids playing and shouting the phrase, "It's not fair." Often, we laugh because we think 3-year-olds do not understand what is fair or unfair in life. Yet, even at a young age, our brains can experience a social threat when treated unfairly. Research has also shown that humans react to unfairness when it's both to our benefit and when it does not benefit us.

Equity is providing everyone with equal access to opportunities and resources. Inclusion efforts in the workplace help to give traditionally marginalized groups, like those based on gender, race or even those with physical or mental disabilities, a means to feel equal in the workplace. Inclusive actions, like creating employee resource groups or hosting information sessions, make the workplace a safer, more respectful environment for all employees. Equity refers to the intentional, ongoing effort to ensure that diverse people with different identities can fully participate in all aspects of the work of an organization, including leadership positions and decision-making processes. It refers to how diverse individuals are valued and respected members and are welcomed in an organization and/or community.

Inclusion

Inclusion is an organizational effort and practice in which different groups or individuals from diverse backgrounds are culturally and socially accepted, welcomed, and equally treated. These differences could be self-evident, such as national origin, age, race and ethnicity, religion/belief, gender, marital status, and socioeconomic status, or they could be more inherent, such as educational background, training, sector experience, organizational tenure and even personality, such as introverts and extroverts.

Inclusive cultures make people feel respected and valued for who they are as individuals or groups. As a result, people feel a level of supportive energy and commitment from others to do their best at work. Inclusion often means a shift in an organization's mindset and culture that has visible effects, such as meeting participation, physical organization offices or access to facilities or information.

The inclusion process engages each individual and makes people feel valued as essential to the organization's success. Evidence shows that when people feel valued, they function at total capacity and feel part of their mission. This culture shift creates higher-performing organizations where motivation and morale soar. Inclusion is an intentional way of creating an environment where all team members can bring their unique selves without the need to mask or assimilate to be accepted. It is about creating a psychologically safe environment where members of the community or workplace feel a sense of belonging. Inclusion is about the human heart because it cannot be measured outside of how the community members feel.

SHRM defines inclusion as "the achievement of a work environment in which all individuals are treated fairly and respectfully, have equal access to opportunities and resources and can contribute fully to the organization's success. Inclusion provides a platform to support and respect employees, which can be expanded to understand and value differences through diversity initiatives. Unfortunately, inclusion in the workplace is often overlooked or wedged in as an afterthought. But an inclusive culture creates a strong foundation for diversity to build on. Inclusion goes beyond supporting and respecting employees—it's about creating a space where employees feel valued, safe, accepted, and heard. Employees should:

- Feel safe to voice their opinions.
- Feel valued as an individual.
- Feel empowered to grow and develop.

Belonging

Janet M. Stovall says the following: The concept of belonging, at best, is subjective. Many of us think about belonging "as being accepted and approved by a group or by society as a whole," according to the American Psychological Association. But, like the grammar of the definition, this belonging-as-sense is passive. It puts the onus of fitting in, on the individual who doesn't fit in.

Another perspective—belonging-as-space—ties the concept to a physical environment where people feel welcome, safe, and free to be authentic. On the surface, belonging-as-space shifts responsibility to the creators of the space. However, the idea, "If you build it, they will belong," doesn't work because people are different, and there's no universal blueprint for building an environment of belonging. Thus, the responsibility shifts back to the individual who needs to belong. The ambiguity begs the question: Which definition is correct?

We can't create a sense of space of belonging for someone else. What we can design, however, are inclusive spaces that allow others to belong. It's a subtle difference that makes the aspirational actionable. Inclusion acknowledges that someone else "owns" the space while promising an intentional effort to expand that space for others by creating psychological safety. As Brian Lowery (associate dean at Stanford University Graduate School of Business) says, The real question is: "To whom does the space belong?" He adds, "Black employees experience stress associated with working in predominantly white workplaces, which contributes to a lower sense of belonging."

Why inclusion is imperative

Research has shown that diverse teams outperform homogeneous teams. The present gap is how we tap into this capability. The answer is inclusion.

Research projects found that in 2030, women will make up 51% of the workforce, we will continue to have 5 generations in the workplace, people of colour will make up over 50% in the USA, and 40% will work remotely and part-time. The workforce will continue to shift dramatically in a wide variety of complexes. Organizations and leaders will need to brand themselves to attract top talent. To attract and retain talent, leaders need to develop muscle on inclusion. People leave bad bosses and toxic environments. John Maxwell expresses it well when he says everything rises and falls on leadership. Leaders have a direct impact on the employee. The global workforce has changed, and so have customer needs.

Work is changing dramatically. We continue to experience changes seen in distributed, digital, and technology-based work. To succeed in these changing environments, a leader needs to embrace reality, care bout the human beings in their charge at an individual level and create an equitable system that removes barriers for marginalized groups and employees.

Broad demographics alone won't make a difference to an organization's bottom line unless the people within those demographics feel authentically welcomed (Gallup, "The No 1 Strategy for True Inclusion in the Workplace"). In other words, leaders need both a diverse workforce *and* an inclusive workplace culture to realize the business benefits of D&I, such as reduced turnover and higher performance.

Why? To excel, employees must feel valued, respected, accepted, and encouraged to fully participate in the organization. In addition, they need to feel recognized for their unique backgrounds, experiences, personalities, and their strength and the things they do exceptionally well. Inclusion only happens when you have a diverse workforce. It also doesn't come only if you have strong leadership promoting diversity but no buy-in from the rest of the organization. As I mentioned, local teams play an equal role in promoting inclusion.

As mentioned earlier, we know millennials define diversity and inclusion much more broadly than previous generations, focusing mainly on demographic differences such as race and gender and other visible demographics. But now, millennials are thinking beyond those demographics and about backgrounds, experiences, and perspectives, which introduces a whole additional layer of diversity. So, in that, managers must find new ways to bridge the gap between all the generations in the workplace. In many organizations, there are four and even five generations in the workplace, which will continue to be exacerbated over the next few years.

So, a few things managers should be thinking about are:

Millennials are such a connected generation. So how do you leverage that level of connection to build more inclusive teams? Are there ways to think beyond the traditional mechanisms of team communication and connection and to leverage that ability to make everyone on the team feel more inclusive, mainly because we believe in remote workers or even remote workers with non-traditional schedules?

Secondly, what we know about millennials is that there is now an expectation of having inclusive conversations. Our technology and social media platforms have allowed people to be much more vocal about their opinions on different issues.

And managers now must be equipped with the tools to have conversations around diversity and inclusion, to talk about some of those challenging things we might see in the news that are happening outside our workplaces. It's no longer OK for managers to skirt the issues and not feel comfortable talking about these conversations anymore, because this new generation of the workforce is going to not only expect to have the conversation; they're also going to look to their managers and leaders to demonstrate some knowledge and care around those topics.

Re-defining Concepts in the Space

As interest and need have grown in diversity, equity, and inclusion, it is becoming more challenging to have an agreed definition of each concept. There are also adverse reactions for people who have felt they are being blamed for the privilege of being born in the majority, creating systemic discrimination. The words also evoke a sense of guilt for some who have sat in sessions and felt it was a finger–pointing game. I have taken time to reflect on the problem and what we are trying to resolve as humanity.

Diversity is about humanity. It is how the 8 billion humans live together on the shared space we named planet Earth. There is one human race. We have the same essential components of what make us human. For example, we all have red and white blood cells. I am yet to meet one that is different. In our most original form, we have the same vital organs: heart, brain, liver, and kidneys. I am not a scientist or biologist, but I understand basic biology. Above all, we all want the same things. I have travelled extensively and met people from everywhere, and everyone wants to have a sense of belonging, to be accepted for their uniqueness and to be welcomed for the common things we share. So, I postulate that diversity is about the human race, the one human race in all its manifestations of being male, female, young, old, black, brown, white, different sexual orientations, wealthy, poor, intelligent, average, tall or short—all these are artificial categories we created for our own reasons.

Equity is about the human brain. The definitions offered above show that equity is about removing barriers and levelling the playing field. To manage that, we need to accept that our brains have been developed and conditioned by the environment and the training we received from a young age. If we have a brain, we are biased. Bias is not the shark; it's the water. Using our brains, we can be aware of those biases that guide us even as we are not consciously aware. Unconscious bias is when the brain defaults to making quick decisions based on the stereotypes and preferences we have developed, saving the brain energy. We are privileged to live in a world where we understand science. Neuroscience and neuroplasticity have taught us that our brains can still change and grow.

Inclusion is about the human heart; we share some fundamental needs. We all want to be loved, to feel that we belong. We have, for the most part, the exact physiological needs. I am yet to meet a person who says they don't want to be loved and accepted for who they are, except the ones whose humanness has been tainted.

CHAPTER THREE

The Human Brain

"Until you make the unconscious conscious,
it will direct your life, and you will call it fate."
– C.G. Jung

Many of us have seen the iceberg analogy, often used to describe the complexity of human culture. To simplify it, it says that whenever we meet another human being, we see 10% of the person's identity through observable things like skin colour, hair texture and language. Ninety per cent of the person is invisible. This includes beliefs, culture, experiences, and many other facets of what makes individuals unique and defines them. The irony is that we make 90% of our judgements based on the 10% of what we see.

What differentiates humans from other animals is the supercomputer between our ears, which we call the brain. The human brain is one of the most fantastic organs on planet Earth. If we look at what the human brain has created, from television to the light bulb, to an aeroplane to a spaceship, so much shows the brain's creative capability and innovative features.

We live in a world of information overload. We receive around 11 million bites of data per second. The conscious brain can process only 40 bites of data per second. The subconscious mind acts as a gatekeeper, enabling us to function without the system crashing. The subconscious mind pulls data and files from the past to make sense of the present.

I have met many people who believe that they have no biases. Some have even told me that they do not see colour. Before I engaged in the work of diversity, equity, and inclusion, I used to be upset and angry with such statements. Now I give people grace because I understand that what they are saying is that they do not intend to be biased consciously. Science has shown us that we are biased if we have a brain. For the most part, we are unaware that our interactions and reactions to people are informed by our deep-seated beliefs and stereotypes. From a brain-science perspective, true objectivity is a myth. We are often unaware of how the lens of our deep beliefs, expectations, fears, and memories colour our view of reality and bypasses sound reasoning. Often, bias is unconscious, outside of our conscious awareness. Liberman says more is needed to do training on bias, in the hope that people can stop bias from affecting their decisions. We are creatures of habit; we need to intentionally work to change our neurons and create new beliefs and habits.

I love the example that Dr. Steven Jones gives. He says the world has many ways and things designed for right-handed people. Right-handed people make up most people on our planet compared to left-handed ones. We have cars, scissors and machines primarily designed for right-handed people. He concludes that when we are a part of the group that makes the majority, our group's way of doing things gets built into the system, is made invisible and is called normal. If left-handed people complain that they are disadvantaged and have barriers, right-handed people will have a hard time recognizing or understanding what the problem could be.

To the brain, similarity equals safety, and to the brain, differences equal potential threats. Understanding these fundamental truths helps understand and humanize bias. We cannot root out bias in our brains. We can mitigate it. The first step to mitigating bias is self-awareness. It is awareness of our physiological and emotional reactions to statements and groups of people. I remember many instances of humbling self-awareness opportunities. I travelled to Heathrow airport, and my connecting flight was from terminal 5. This is where most flights to the Middle East and some African destinations leave from. When I saw many people dressed in clothes that suggested they could be Muslim, my mind was gripped by fear. I paid attention to it and interrogated the fear. I feared someone might have a bomb. I had to do a lot of self-talk and talk my mind out of the unfounded fear that every Muslim has a bomb and plans to hijack a plane. I realized that the 911 event had left unresolved biases and fear in me. I had to remind myself that I practice curiosity in the face of differences. So as soon as I went through the security gate, I sat next to a woman wearing a hijab and started a conversation. She had a fascinating story. I forgot about my fears.

The question that has baffled our minds is, "How is it possible that so many well-intentioned and kind people continue to be biased and cause pain and hurt to others? Research has shown that the answer is our biology, the human brain. But unfortunately, we are often unaware of how the lens of our beliefs, experiences, expectations, and fears taint our view of reality and bypass our objective reasoning.

For the most part, our brains have a way of memorizing past decisions and having them provide shortcuts for future similar decisions. Thus, unconscious bias is sometimes good. It helps save energy and the brain from exhaustion when navigating through complex chunks of information to make decisions. For example, once we learn to drive, we do not have to think hard each time we jump into a car to go somewhere. But, on the other hand, sometimes we get to a place and wonder how we got there as we shift gears, stop, and move automatically with the change of lights.

The downside to our brains operating on saved memories is that the subconscious does not differentiate between truth and falsity. It believes in stereotypes. For example, the stereotypes enforced through historical systems that Indigenous people are savages that need to be civilized, or black people are not human and can be enslaved. Our subconscious minds will work at isolating and avoiding those groups that are different from us and based on negative stereotypes. As a manager in a hiring position, you can see how it would be easy to hire people like you, because your brain will take shortcuts in decision-making. For example, associating men with high IQs or competence, associating Indians with high IQs in maths and science, that Jews seek to dominate humanity, or associating women with jobs like cleaning, nursing, and cooking.

The danger with unconscious bias is that more than just discriminating against people based on our beliefs and stereotypes, sometimes such beliefs fueled by fear can develop into some form of hate or extremism. I discuss examples of extremism in another chapter. People have asked the question, if I am unaware of the biases that influence decision-making, how can I be held accountable for them? This is a good question. However, it's not a blame game. It is a human issue that needs to be resolved. Humans are creatures of habit, and we thrive on detecting danger and running into what we perceive to be safe. We like routine and predictability. Awareness is key when it comes to mitigating unconscious bias.

Research has identified over 150 biases that our brains produce and rely on. I will only discuss some, as this will take another book, but I will focus on a few as examples. Research has shown that social exclusion has been shown to activate the brain in a similar way to experiencing physical pain (Eisenberger, Lieberman, and Williams, 2003). The brain is thus highly reactive to social inclusion and exclusion. As far as the brain is concerned, social rejection hurts. Social exclusion is why we saw the surge in mental health issues during COVID-19. The lesson that we involuntarily learned during the pandemic is that despite our socially constructed categories of race, gender, and many others, we are all humans whose lives are designed on the need to belong and for social inclusion.

While research shows the obvious, the question is, if exclusion has these harmful effects, why would anyone exclude others? The answer is that we accidentally exclude others in ways most of us are unaware of. I have heard many people say that they have not met anyone who wakes up and intentionally plans to screw the system or give others a hard time in the workplace. This is primarily true for most people except for those who might be in a different mental state or have lost their humanity. The exclusionary behaviour we all sometimes display is often insidious and more driven by the subconscious mind than the conscious mind. These exclusionary behaviours are usually informed by general stereotypes and prejudices we hold. Exclusionary behaviours have been commonly described as "microaggressions" (Sue et al. I, 2007). Often, the person displaying microaggressions does not know they are doing it. For example, colleagues have asked me frequently, "Where did you learn your English?" I used to struggle to respond to the question and was tempted to react and ask why they were asking me such a foolish question. Now I respond with sarcasm and say I was taught English by the British; they colonized Zimbabwe just as Canada was also occupied by the British. I usually get some awkward laughs and reactions to my sarcasm.

Another example is that as a black woman, I am privileged to be able to do many funky styles with my hair. I can have it as a natural afro, corn roll it, braid it or have extensions weaved in. Yet, I often get asked if this is my natural hair. Or I get people asking if they can touch my hair. Then I think to myself that I would never have the audacity to ask to touch another woman's hair unless I was their hairdresser. Nor would I ever ask my colleagues if their natural hair was curly or straight, or if the green or whatever colour they dyed their hair was real or fake.

I remember, in one organization, where I was at the table but never truly included. I often got the phrase, "We will let you know." This was a clear message that there was an ingroup, and I was not part of it. It also told me that the decisions would be made without me, and I would be told what to do. In the same organization, I realized many times that when we came to the table, decisions were already made, deliberations were done, and the meeting was to rubber stamp what was discussed and agreed on outside of the formal meeting. Often, the ideas were presented by one and quickly followed by the "I agree" from the rest of the team. Finally, I was still trying to process the concept given, and the decision was passed.

One of my recent experiences has been the observation that people do not look me in the eye. I come from a culture were looking an elder in the eye is considered disrespectful. I made a conscious effort to learn to look people in the eye. I also learnt that in some Indigenous cultures in Canada, looking someone in the eye is disrespectful because the eyes are considered windows to the soul. I am not talking about the Shona or Indigenous culture; I am talking about working with Caucasians who know and believe that looking someone in the eye is a sign of respect and presence. People will come and give me instructions and never look at me. They leave my office, go to another Caucasian next door, start a conversation, and look each other in the eye. I have reflected on what the driver could be and recognized that the subconscious mind is strong, and stereotypes are real. Here I am, a black immigrant woman, and automatically I am the "other" in that person's brain. While eye contact signals warmth and inclusion, avoiding eye contact, as I often experience, can conversely signal disinterest and exclusion. With this background information on the bias, I will discuss some common biases, I will not attempt to discuss all 150 but will discuss a few in this chapter to illustrate how our brains work.

Similarity Bias

Similarity bias, also called affinity bias, refers to the desire to work with people that look like you or that share commonalities with you. Humans tend to see themselves and those similar in a favourable light—people who grew up in the same neighborhoods went to the same school as us, and the list continues. To the brain, the familiar feels safe, and anything different is a potential threat. Therefore, we instinctively create ingroups and outgroups. In the work sphere, this translates into them and us. Instead of looking at a different person as an opportunity to meet and develop a relationship or collaborate, our brain tells us to protect ourselves because something unfamiliar threatens us.

As you can see, this is not an issue limited to race or gender, as it is traditionally associated with cases of differences. Instead, it is about how our human brains are wired to protect us. Therefore, the best of us are biased even without us being aware or intending to be.

Expedience Bias

We live in a world where life moves fast, and things change quickly. As humans, we have a deep-seated need for certainty. Expedience bias is taking mental shortcuts that help us make quick and efficient decisions based on accessible information. We default to such shortcuts when juggling many tasks, are under tight deadlines and are spread so thin that we perceive that we have no time. The brain takes mental shortcuts in a world of information overload and many what-ifs. As a result, it defaults to energy-saving and intuitive systems.

Experience Bias

This type of bias occurs when we fail to remember that we all view the world not as it is but as we are. We do not hold the same worldview and experience the world around us uniquely. These differences are not about right or wrong; they are different. Unfortunately, our brains are designed to perceive our immediate environment as an accurate representation of reality.

Distance Bias

We talked about how, to the brain, anything familiar is safety, and anything different is a threat. Distance bias reveals our instinct to prioritize what is nearby. This bias was evident in my experience where we already were a virtual team before COVID-19. My colleagues who had offices at the same site as our boss, had the boss's ear and often would get information before the rest of us. Now that most of us work remotely, this bias manifest itself in meetings. For example, people in the same room often engage in inside conversations, and people sitting remotely feel isolated and excluded. As we move into the world of remote and hybrid work, managers must learn new skills to be inclusive. As a leader, one of the ways to mitigate such bias is always calling the people furthest from you to contribute first.

Safety Bias

This bias refers to the human tendency to avoid loss. The brain is more sensitive to potential loss than potential gains. In other words, any sense of bad in our minds is more substantial than good.

Other biases include:

Name bias – Selecting someone for a job or an interview based on their name and likely heritage.

Beauty bias – Preferring to work with people that are considered pleasing to the eye or more attractive.

Height bias –Ostracizing someone who is not a standard height, because they don't look like everyone else. Size correlates directly to leadership potential, power, strength, and intelligence.

Exclusion fuels the fear of difference. Inclusion, on the other hand, fuels acceptance. Since the 1980s, studies have shown that people can act in biased ways despite explicitly believing that prejudice and discrimination are wrong. This is because of unconscious bias. It is insidious and perpetuates stereotypes in our brains. This bias is also why there has yet to be much progress across sectors and institutions in all types of equity. Individuals and systems are intrinsically biased.

The first step is awareness. The second step is mitigating the bias, which is a lot of work, and it takes humility to catch oneself and rewire the brain differently.

Let us use one example of the "war between the generations." The baby boomers believe that the millennials are lazy, entitled, and non-committal. If Generation Z comes to a baby boomer with a question, it triggers the defensiveness in the brain: "Here we go again; always asking why and not taking direction and having an excuse not to work." This young person has a genuine question, wants to learn or is looking for more efficient ways to have systems and processes. In this example, diversity of thought has been dismissed, and innovation thwarted.

We can flip the coin and find a similar example. Millennials believe that the baby boomers are set in their ways and lack techno-savviness. Any attempt to ask a question and suggest that there are processes that have been tried and tested and work just fine, and we do not need to fix them if they are broken, will be considered being set in one's ways and resisting change.

If bias is unconscious and we cannot eradicate it completely, how can we reduce it? Many people ask this question, and I have asked the same myself. I am sharing in this book what has worked for me. Besides science, lived experiences can help as well. The first step is to destigmatize bias and accept it as part of being human. The examples I have given in this chapter of instances where I found myself reacting or making decisions based on my brain taking a shortcut, I have used the technique of interrogating my feelings or judgments. Knowing that

43

biases are a human and normal function of my brain has encouraged me to do the inner work that sharpens my self-awareness. The recognition that bias is natural also helped me give grace to others. Finally, labelling my biases helps me mitigate them by avoiding expedient decisions and considering options and consequences before deciding.

CHAPTER FOUR

Hate, Extremism and Bias

"To deny people their humanity is challenging their humanity."
– Nelson Mandela

Around the world, we are seeing a disturbing groundswell of xenophobia, racism, and intolerance, including rising antisemitism, anti-Muslim hatred, anti-black racism, and persecution of Christians. Social media and other forms of communication are being exploited as platforms for bigotry. Neo-Nazi and white supremacy movements are on the march. Public discourse is being weaponized for political gain with incendiary rhetoric that stigmatizes and dehumanizes minorities, migrants, refugees, women and any so-called "others." I often reflect on the quote by John Milton, which says that "the mind in its place and itself can make a heaven out of hell, or hell of heaven."

Hate crimes and incidents are rising globally, and Canada is no exception. A hate crime is a criminal incident that is found to have been motivated by hatred toward an identifiable person or group. Such groups can be distinguished by race, national or ethnic origin, language, colour of skin, religion, sex, age, mental or physical disability, sexual orientation, or gender identity.

Hate propaganda is the promotion of hatred against identifiable groups. The goal is to portray a group as inferior and/or dangerous. In an extreme case, hatred of the "other" can be carried out within a political process, as was with Nazi Germany, or can be a tribal war, as was with Rwanda. The typical irony is that the perpetrators often feel like victims themselves, acting in self-defence. Often, the perpetrators use simple and untested information for complex problems. For example, in South Africa, as the economy suffers and starts to slide down, South Africans look to blame foreigners and lash out with xenophobic attacks. To that extent, hate mongers are often motivated by conspiracy theories. Technology and the internet have enabled the spread of conspiracy theories and recent events, such as Trump's allegations that the elections were fake, and conspiracy theories about the origins of the coronavirus or the vaccine.

Hate grows in silence and feeds on indifference. Silence is when we refuse to question our own biases. Left unchecked, hatred incubates; and left for too long, hate flourishes. Far too often, we have seen insecurity growing. Places of worship are traditionally associated with peace and safety. Still, the Quebec, Canada shooting that killed 7 people in a mosque in January 2017, and the shooting in Christchurch, New Zealand, which left 51 dead and 40 injured, to name but a few, has shown us that there is no safety. A grocery store is where anyone with money can purchase groceries without fear of being gunned down. Still, on May 14, 2022, the shooting of 10 people in a Tops grocery store in a predominately black community in Buffalo, New York, demonstrates that hate-motivated crimes are rife. Ten days after the shooting in Buffalo, New York, 19 students and two teachers were gunned down at Robb Elementary School in Texas. Schools are places where teachers and students are allowed to learn without fear of losing their lives.

Similarly, nightclubs and concerts are places where humans traditionally gather to enjoy life through music, dance, and drinks. Still, recently, these places have been targeted for "message crimes" and incidents. Hate is based on fear, often unfounded and based on categorizations that see others as a demographic threat. This is what Islamophobia, antisemitism, anti-Asian, anti-black and many other categories use. Unfortunately, these categories continue to put communities in harm's way.

Hate crimes are criminal violations committed against a person or property, motivated in whole or part by an offender's bias, prejudice or hatred toward a certain actual or perceived characteristic of a victim's identity. These crimes attack guaranteed rights and freedoms and erode shared values of equality, freedom, and respect for all individuals. Hate-motivated crimes and incidents pose a persistent public safety risk, as they undermine social cohesion and inclusion and perpetuate division and categorization. On May 25, 2022, I was appointed by the Government of Alberta as one of the two first-ever appointed hate crime community liaisons. The area of hate crime is something I am passionate about. It is a complex area, and I will not dive deeper into the discussion. My goal is to show that if our bias and prejudice are not checked, they can grow and produce intense feelings of hate that instills fear and paralyzes our ability to live together in harmony as humans.

Hatred is the emotional state of intense hostility caused by a perceived threat. It is a sentiment of intense animosity or hostility toward an individual or a group. It is a passionate and dangerous emotion—a complete loss of one's boundaries in the presence of someone living out their shadow. A profound mirror communicates what is missing, unfinished or unwelcome inside someone. Psychologists like Freud have talked about the process of projecting. It is a defence mechanism in which the ego defends itself against disowned and highly negative parts of the self by denying their existence in themselves and attributing them to others; it is the human ego in a state of defence. Humans are as violent as they are brilliant. The more we feel safe, the less hate we think. At its root, hatred occurs when we feel powerless. It is when we feel powerless that we act out. Hatred aims at eliminating its target.

In this book, I adopt Barbra Perry's definition that hate crimes are acts of violence and intimidation, usually directed toward already stigmatized and marginalized groups. As such, hate crimes are a mechanism of power intended to reaffirm the precarious hierarchies that characterize a given social order. It attempts to recreate the threatened (real or imagined) hegemony of the perpetrator's group and the appropriate subordinate identity of the victim's group (Perry, 2001). This definition demonstrates that hate crimes and incidents are driven by fear of losing power within an established system.

Michele Grossman et al. (2016) conducted a systematic review of research, between 2011 and 2015, to find risk factors for violent extremism. The study identified a diverse set of elements in the literature by looking at the so-called root causes of terrorism, mainly structural and group-level factors. Furthermore, the researchers identified a list of factors that influence or lead to violent extremism, which includes a list of *sub-cultural factors* (such as boundaries of identity and belonging and oppositional sub-cultures of resistance) and *experiential factors* (such as the desire for excitement and the search for meaning and glory). Moreover, *social media* plays a role in sourcing information, propaganda, and social interactions online, and this constitutes a new environment where radicalization mechanisms can occur.

I will give examples of what happens when bias and extremism go unchecked.

The slave trade was a heinous practice showing the ugly head of racism. Several films and stories have been written about Slave Trade. Among them are *The Color Purple*, *Selma*, and *Roots*. They show how our human brains can be conditioned to commit deplorable crimes and justify them. I mention these defining moments in recent history, not to make anybody feel guilty but to show how perverse our minds and hearts can be if they go unchecked.

The Nazi and Jewish Holocaust

It began with a simple boycott of Jewish shops. It ended in the gas chambers of Auschwitz as Hitler and his Nazi followers attempted to exterminate the entire Jewish population of Europe. The Holocaust took the lives of nearly six million Jews during World War II. Antisemitism was the central component of Nazi ideology. Also murdered millions of Poles, Russians, Roma, Sinti, Serbs, Czechs, homosexuals and political opponents, Jews were slated for total annihilation. The "final solution" was partially successful through the process of genocide. The Nazi Party targeted the Jews, isolated them into ghettos and deported their victims to concentration camps where most perished. Others became Nazi victims, not because of who they were but because of what they did—Jehovah's Witnesses, the dissenting clergy, communists, socialists, and other political enemies. Antisemitism has long been called the world's "oldest hatred," as it has existed in one form or another since antiquity. Justifications for antisemitisms range from malicious accusations against Jews and Judaism, from far-right antisemitism, informed by (dis)utopian ideologies that label Jews as malignant actors seeking to dominate humanity, to far-left antisemitisms that targets Jews under the guise of criticism of the State of Israel, and so forth. If one thing can be said about antisemitisms, it is that it is a malleable prejudice. To delineate the parameters of antisemitisms and identify its root causes, B'nai Brith Canada uses the International Holocaust Remembrance Alliance (IHRA) Working Definition of Antisemitism, the world's most expert and consensus-driven definition of antisemitisms, and the exact definition used by the Government of Canada, the Governments of Alberta, Ontario and New Brunswick and an increasing number of municipalities across the country. IHRA is an intergovernmental organization formed in 1998 to unite governments and experts to advance and promote Holocaust education.

Bosnia-Herzegovina – The Mass Murder of Muslims

In the Republic of Bosnia-Herzegovina, the conflict between the three main ethnic groups—the Serbs, Croats, and Muslims—resulted in genocide committed by the Serbs, against Bosnian Muslims. In the late 1980s, a Serbian named Slobodan Milosevic came to power. In 1992, acts of "ethnic cleansing" started in Bosnia, a primarily Muslim country where the Serb minority made up only 32% of the population. Milosevic responded to Bosnia's declaration of independence by attacking Sarajevo, where Serb snipers shot down civilians. The Bosnian Muslims were outgunned, and the Serbs continued to gain ground. They systematically rounded up local Muslims and committed acts of mass murder, deported men and boys to concentration camps and forced the repopulation of entire towns. Serbs also terrorized Muslim families by using rape as a weapon against women and girls. Over 200,000 Muslim civilians were systematically murdered, and 2,000,000 became refugees at the hands of the Serbs. Hate-motivated crimes and extremism can lead to egregious acts, as described above.

Gukurahundi – Zimbabwe Ethnic-Tribal Genocide

The Gukurahundi was a series of massacres of Ndebele civilians, carried out by the Zimbabwe National Army, from early 1983 to late 1987. It derives from a Shona language term, which loosely translates to "the early rain that washes away the chaff before the spring rains." During the Rhodesian liberation war, two rival nationalist parties, Robert Mugabe's Zimbabwe African National Union (ZANU), and Joshua Nkomo's Zimbabwe African People's Union (ZAPU), emerged to challenge Rhodesia's predominantly white government. ZANU initially defined Gukurahundi as an ideological strategy to carry the war into major settlements and individual homesteads. However, following Mugabe's ascension to power, his government remained threatened by "dissidents"—disgruntled former guerrillas and supporters of ZAPU. The ruling party recruited mainly from Shona people, whereas the ZAPU had its greatest support among the minority Ndebele. In early 1983, the North Korean-trained Fifth Brigade began a crackdown on dissidents in Matabeleland and Midlands, the homelands of the Ndebele. Over the following two years, thousands of Ndebele were detained by government forces and either marched to re-education camps or summarily executed. Although there are different estimates, the consensus of the International Association of Genocide Scholars, or IAGS, is that more than 20,000 people were killed. The IAGS has classified the massacres as genocide.

Rwanda, Case of Ethnic Genocide

Beginning on April 6, 1994, groups of ethnic Hutu, armed mostly with machetes, started a campaign of terror and bloodshed, embroiling the Central African country of Rwanda. For about 100 days, the Hutu militias, known in Rwanda as Interahamwe, followed what evidence suggests was a clear and premeditated attempt to exterminate the country's ethnic Tutsi population. The Rwandan state radio, controlled by Hutu extremists, further encouraged the killings by broadcasting non-stop hate propaganda and even pinpointed the locations of Tutsis in hiding. The massacre ended after armed Tutsi rebels, invading from neighbouring countries, defeated the Hutus and halted the genocide in July 1994. By then, over one-tenth of the population, an estimated 800,000 persons, had been killed. In addition, the country's industrial infrastructure had been destroyed, and much of its population had been dislocated.

To the brain, anything different from us poses a threat. This is how animals survive predators. Given the examples above of what hate can do if not checked, let us investigate the cause of hatred. Psychology and neuroscience have shared that hate usually stems from fear. Psychologists like Carl Young and Sigmund Freud say that generally, as humans, we hate people who display things we do not like in ourselves. Projection is placing your negative traits or unwanted emotions onto others, usually without reason—**the mental process by which people attribute to others what is in their minds**. There are different reasons why people feel hatred, such as having a fear of vulnerability or a fear of facing their own identity. When you feel that intense emotion of hatred, it is a complete loss of your boundaries; it is a form of holding a mirror to your shadow, seeing things you hate about yourself. Hatred reveals to me what is missing, unfinished or unwelcome in myself.

Experts say that chronic hatred and extreme anger can add to stress and affect our physical and mental health. Apply that to a business, and the results are financially devastating. The cycle is deadly. Psychologists say that carrying hostility around can kill us. Wishing evil to someone does more damage to us than to the objects of our anger and hatred. No one is born a violent extremist; they are made and fueled. Disarming the radicalization process must begin with human rights and the rule of law, with dialogue across all boundary lines, empowering all young women and men, and starting as early as possible on the benches of schools.

It is important to note that if we are human, we risk experiencing the intense emotion of hate. If we do not deal with our shadow self and build a solid moral structure within ourselves, it is easy to slide and become the hater. We are as much a violent species as we are brilliant. While this paints a dark side of human emotions, the good news is that we can create awareness and avoid extremism. Hatred is the human ego in a state of defence, and to be in a state of defence, means there is perceived or real fear. In most instances, it is perceived fear. Here are a few ways we can avoid hatred. Some cultural practices also promote division and, if unchecked, hatred.

First, we need to question our feelings of perceived threat. We know that our brains are designed to protect us; hence, we feel the flight or fight reactions to different situations. The first step is to interrogate our fears. Question if our perceived fears are based on facts. The ability to question our fears requires vulnerability and honesty with ourselves. It is an exercise that requires one to be comfortable with challenging oneself and questioning one's wired beliefs. I will give you an example of my shadow and projection that I was unaware of for a long time. A friend of mine loved tennis and adored Serena Williams. Whenever he shared his excitement about Serena winning tournaments, I would remind him that I would not say I liked Serena; instead, I preferred her sister Venus. It was only when I started doing inner work on myself and asked why I would not say I liked Serena, and when I questioned my feelings and thoughts about Serena, that I discovered she had accomplished what I could not. Growing up, I was athletic, and my parents were more focused on the academic side of our education. I realized then that I considered myself a strong woman and did not like to see another successful black woman who was strong. It took courage for me to face myself and confront my ego.

The second strategy we must use is increasing our sense of safety. I can use a typical example of immigrants and refugees. Many people who hate immigrants perceive their jobs, place and well-being as threatened as the newcomers will displace them. It is a perceived fear.

I grew up in Zimbabwe, and we had immigrants from Malawi, Mozambique, and Rwanda. We were socialized to look down upon these immigrants as they were doing the jobs that most Zimbabweans did not like. They worked in the mines, on the farms and as domestic workers. In retrospect, I see how these immigrants enriched our culture and contributed to our economy. At that time, Zimbabwe was known as the breadbasket of Africa, and 60% of the farm workers were immigrants. I look at the 20 years that I have lived in Canada and see how hard I have worked and contributed to the communities that I have lived in. Unfortunately, from time to time, I watch xenophobic attacks in South Africa, where they are against foreigners. I am saddened by the intensity of hate and resentment that drives people to take the law into their hands and burn people alive. Such egregious acts can only happen when we allow fear to dismantle all safety boundaries around us and play the victim card.

The third strategy in dealing with feelings of hate is to take care of our mental health. As mentioned before, no one is born a hater, yet no one is immune to bias, hatred, and extremism. How about choosing to treat differences with empathy and kindness? Remember that some things in this life make this world small and connected. Let kindness be one of them.

In my engagement with the community, one gap became apparent. When it comes to hate crimes and incidents, there are four groups of people involved: the perpetrator, the victim, the community, and the system that deals with the crime or incident. Within the Canadian justice system, when an act is committed, the victim or people around the victim place a 911 call to report it. The incident is assigned to the police for response and investigation. The police complete their investigations and pass them on to the Crown prosecutors, who can lay charges. In deciding to prosecute, crown prosecutors will assess if there is a substantial likelihood of conviction and, if so, whether the public interest requires a prosecution. Understanding this process helps the public to have confidence in the system. Other alternative responses can be accessed when an act does not does not meet the threshold in the criminal code no criminal charges can be laid, the victim lose trust in the system.

One issue that has become apparent with hate crimes and incidents is the intersectionality of identities. For example, one can be a disabled lesbian woman or a black Muslim woman. When the law requires a person to pick one identity as to why they were targeted, that presents an identity crisis and a hierarchy of grounds for protection. As hate crimes and incidents of harassment rise, marginalized groups have noticed that there is more strength in coming together to fight hate, than in silo interventions. Traditionally, groups would be categorized as either religious or racially targeted, and then gender and sexual orientation. With the intersectionality of identities, there is more recognition of the need to come together as marginalized communities and victims. This recent shift will mitigate the issues of hierarchy groups that have naturally grown from how legislation has been formed and evolving.

A recent study published by the Department of Justice Canada examined how Canadian courts have applied hate as an aggravating factor at sentencing, using subparagraph 718.2(a)(i) of the Criminal Code. I find the following findings of the study quite revealing. First, the average age of hate crime offenders was about 31 years old, and offences committed by male offenders made up most of the case law reviewed; in only a tiny minority of cases, a female was the principal perpetrator. In the case law reviewed, offenders identified as white were the most frequent offenders. Hatred against race, nationality or ethnicity is the most common motivating factor recorded in published case law. Within case law dealing with racial hatred, the Arab population was the most targeted, followed by the black people; this information was corroborated in police-reported hate crime statistics. Fourth, in both police-reported hate crimes and published case law, hate crimes committed on the grounds of religion were the second most frequent grounds of victimization. In the reviewed case law, the Muslim population was the most targeted religious group, followed by the Jewish people.

One of the sad facts revealed is that young people are mostly the ones who are perpetrators. Despite the strides made by globalization and digitalization, racism continues to show its ugly head in different generations. Crimes motivated by prejudice and bias, based on race, nationality, and ethnicity, show that as a human race, until and unless we learn to accept our differences and stop seeing those different from us as a demographic threat, we will not be truly civilized or liberated. There have been a lot of acknowledgements that we need a systemic change; the systems in place are not broken and were designed to enhance the racial divide. I also add that the starting point is our families. How we raise our children contributes immensely to the citizens we bring up and the culture we build. We can honestly check ourselves and reflect on what we teach our children and our conversations in our homes.

One of the practices that have helped me deal with my own fears, prejudice and bias is curiosity. I was privileged to study philosophy and world religions in my first degree. I learnt about different schools of thought, from Plato to Aristotle, to Socrates, to Frederick Nietzsche, to Emmanuel Kant, to David Hume. During my philosophical studies, I learnt that people could see the world differently, as did Plato and Aristotle, but need not hate or kill each other for having different beliefs and perspectives. Studying world religions helped me understand the concept of religious pluralism. The idea is that no one religion holds the truth; each religion, be it Christianity, Islam, Hinduism, Jewish or other traditional religions, holds a fraction of the facts.

CHAPTER FIVE

Groups That Usually Feel Excluded

*"We tend to avoid the uncomfortable. We can't change what we
don't understand. And we can't possibly know what we avoid."*
– Author Unknown

Racialized Groups/Minority Groups

The Britannica defines racism, also called racialism, as the belief
that humans may be divided into separate and exclusive
biological entities called "races"; that there is a causal link
between inherited physical traits and traits of personality, intel-
lect, morality, and other cultural and behavioural features; and that
some races are innately superior to others. The term is also applied
to political, economic, or legal institutions and systems that engage in
or perpetuate discrimination based on race or otherwise reinforce
racial inequalities in wealth and income, education, health care, civil
rights and other areas. Since the late 20th century, biological race has
been recognized as a cultural invention without a scientific basis.

Racism was at the heart of North American slavery and Western
European colonization and empire-building activities, especially in the

18th century. The idea of race was invented to magnify the differences between people of European origin and those of African descent whose ancestors had been involuntarily enslaved and transported to the Americas.

There is no fixed definition of racial discrimination. However, it has been described as any distinction, conduct or action, whether intentional or not, but based on a person's race, which has the effect of imposing burdens on an individual or group, not imposed upon others or which withholds or limits access to benefits available to other members of society. Race need only be a factor for racial discrimination to have occurred.

Recognizing that race is a social construct, common lexicon now describes people as "racialized persons" or "racialized groups" instead of the more outdated and inaccurate terms of "racial minority," "visible minority," "person of colour," or "non-white."

Racism is a broader phenomenon than racial discrimination. While most countries seek to combat racism through public education and the advancement of human rights, not every manifestation of racism can be dealt with through the current human rights complaint mechanism and process. Nevertheless, racism plays a significant role in fostering racial discrimination.

Racism is an ideology that either directly or indirectly asserts that one group is inherently superior to others. It can be openly displayed in racial jokes and slurs or hate crimes, but it can be more deeply rooted in attitudes, values, and stereotypical beliefs. In some cases, these are unconsciously held and have become deeply embedded in systems and institutions that have evolved over time. Racism operates at several levels: individual, systemic, and societal.

Racism is different from racial prejudice, hatred, or discrimination. Racism involves one group having the power to carry out systematic discrimination through society's institutional policies and practices, and by shaping the cultural beliefs and values that support those racist policies and procedures.

Racism claims the human species can be divided into different biological groups that determine the behaviour, economic and political success of individuals within that group. This belief views races as natural and fixed subdivisions of the human species, each with its distinct and variable cultural characteristics and capacity for developing civilizations. Thus, racists believe that biological factors can be used to explain the social and cultural variations of humans. Racism also includes the belief that there is a natural hierarchical ordering of groups of people so that superior races can dominate inferior ones.

Racist thinking presumes that differences among groups are innate and not subject to change. Thus, intelligence, attitudes and beliefs are viewed as not affected by one's environment or history. The existence of groups at the bottom or top of the social hierarchy is interpreted as the natural outcome of an inferior or superior biological makeup and not the result of social influences. Racists reject social integration because they believe mixing groups would result in the degeneration of the superior group.

If biological differences are not easily discernible, racists invent biological differences (for example, the size of the nose or the colour of the eyes). Racism does not exist because of objective, physical differences among humans, but rather because of the social recognition and the importance of such differences.

Racist ideology is based upon two false assumptions: Biological differences are equal to cultural differences, and biological makeup determines a group's cultural achievements. That biological makeup limits the type of culture a group can develop. Research shows these assumptions are wrong and based mainly on the untenable position that biology is the single cause for everything. Evidence showing that differences within groups are more significant than differences between groups, and that social factors impact behaviour, argues strongly against racist beliefs.

As mentioned earlier, the impact of COVID-19 has been worse for some groups, including racialized communities. Although race-based data are not consistently available globally, local sources indicate that racialized communities are disproportionately impacted by COVID-19. These disproportionate impacts among racialized and Indigenous communities are not due to biological differences between groups or populations. Instead, they reflect existing health inequities strongly influenced by specific social and economic determinants, such as income, education, employment, and housing.

Members of racialized communities were more likely to experience inequitable living and working conditions that make them more susceptible to COVID-19, such as lower incomes, precarious employment, overcrowded housing and limited health and social services. For example, many care providers in long-term care facilities in Canadian cities are racialized women. In addition, racialized employees comprise a significant component of Canadian agriculture and food production systems. The working conditions in these facilities, higher risk living conditions at home and the use of public transport are all factors that put these employees at an increased risk for COVID-19.

Franz Boaz was seen as uniquely different rather than civilized or not civilized. I am not less intelligent or primitive; I am just far from home—cultural relativity. Africans, Asians, and Europeans all have different origins. Why does the myth of multiple human races persist, with multiple racial categories? All humans are members of a single species, the Homo sapiens. Genetic variations do not necessarily correlate with the racialized categories of Hispanic, Asian, African, or Caucasian.

Much like gender, the race is just as much a social contract. *The Bridge over the Racial Divide: Rising Inequality and Coalition Politics* says something profound. It says that racism is an ideology of racial domination at the root. The presumed biological or cultural superiority of one or more racial groups is used to justify or prescribe the inferior treatment or social positions of other racial groups. "Race" is generally understood as a social construct among social scientists. The scientific consensus is that race is not a biological category among humans. This social construction of race has unleashed the division of humanity. "Race" was first used to describe peoples and societies—what we now understand as ethnicity or national identity. Then, Western colonialism and slavery expanded, and the concept was used to justify and prescribe exploitation, domination and violence against people who were racialized as non-white.

I was born during the colonial era and at the height of the liberation war in Rhodesia. Rhodesia was colonized by the British around 1891. There was white domination and, as a young girl, my idea of race was baked through the lens of an occupied and marginalized society. When the British colonized that part of the world, they moved the locals to less desirable land. They called it "reserves," much like the apartheid system in South Africa, where black people were pushed into less desirable areas, which were then coined as "Bantustans." The colonizers occupied the best land and lived in the cities. Black people were primarily domestic workers, farmworkers and labourers in the mines and construction. Everything white was deemed excellent and superior, and black was associated with evil, ugly, witchcraft and bad luck. Thus, the social construct of race carries with it some connotations of intellectual, spiritual, moral, and other forms of superiority, which are systemically constructed into societies to justify the domination of Europeans over racialized others. When I moved to Canada, I found the same system where Indigenous people lived in the periphery outside the mainstream. They lived on tribal lands called the "reserves."

I have often wondered why a person born of both a white and a black parent, or any other non-Caucasian parent, is called black. When Obama became president, there was a celebration of the first black president, and I kept saying to my friends that he was not black; he is mixed. Why is he not allowed to choose how he wants to identify himself?

I have been saddened by the many times that I have been told that female lawyers should expect to be treated with less respect or even harassed by their male colleagues in the legal system. To my horror, I represented a client who needed help recovering the money he was owed. The person who owed them money was belligerent and used bullying and harassment tactics to scare people away from litigating. This bully called me all sorts of names in a court setting and was not held to account. It bothered me, and I sent a letter to the presiding justice of peace expressing my disappointment and that we should feel safe and protected by the system as lawyers. There should be zero tolerance for abuse. Instead, I was again told that I should expect clients to be rude to female lawyers. As much as the world has progressed, we still have a long way to go to respect women and other groups. As a black immigrant woman, the intersectionality of gender, race, nationality, and ethnicity all expose me to different types of discrimination and marginalization.

Jane Elliot is one of the people known in present history who fought against racism. In her own words, she encouraged schoolchildren to refuse to perpetuate the myth of white superiority. There is one race, the human race. In her famous exercise, popularly known as "the blue eyes, brown eyes experience," aired on different channels, she asked some poignant questions: Do white people want to be treated the way black people are treated? Honestly, no one wants to be treated as less human; however, when one's group is in power, there is a subconscious need to guard and protect one's privilege. Privilege does not begin and end in racism. I have been in many spaces of privilege, too, and it takes awareness to recognize and accept it without being defensive.

It's time to get over the myth that we have 5 human races.. In school, we get indoctrinated. Education is meant to lead a person out of ignorance. Still, most education systems have led us into ignorance and perpetuated the falsity that some races are superior to others. Racism is so perverse; racism, based on a lie, is idiocy. Power never willingly conceded to the powerless, naturally. The fear is that if the tables turn, the racialized groups will treat white people the same way they were treated.

The Story of Indigenous People in Canada

Historically, Indigenous people in Canada were called Indios because the Spaniards used that term. They have been called Indians, Natives, Aboriginals and Indigenous throughout the years. Before colonization, Indigenous people lived in this country as a complex collection of nations with their own structures, history, and lifestyle. To understand Indigenous people, it is crucial to comprehend their own history and culture.

Residential schools were created through a government assimilation policy meant to remove the "Indian" from Indigenous children. The belief was that removing native languages and culture was necessary for colonization. As a result, thousands of Indigenous children were removed from their families and forcibly taken into residential schools. Residential schools effectively destroyed the cultures and traditions of Indigenous people as these were based on oral traditions. In addition, children were abused, and trans-generational trauma was created. The recent discoveries of mass graves at former residential schools in Canada are the tip of the iceberg of the abuses that both the government, the Catholic, and Anglican Churches inflicted on the Indigenous communities of Canada.

In both the US and Canada, these boarding schools were founded on the motto, "Kill the Indian to save the man." The schools were mandatory for Native children and forced their assimilation into Western culture. Unfortunately, this genocidal policy was veiled as education, and the practice, regardless of intentions, resulted in the abuse, neglect and robbing of Native children from their homes, families, and culture.

Boarding schools were an instrument in executing the token United States dream—manifest destiny—as it promoted expansion, imperialism and Western culture through decimating and belittling the Native way of life. Students were forbidden from speaking their native languages, wearing traditional clothing, or practicing their way of life. Instead, they were forced to practice Christianity and leave their spiritualities and customs behind. The goal of the boarding schools was to *"eradicate all vestiges of Indian culture."*

The Sixties Scoop is the catch-all name for a series of policies enacted by provincial child welfare authorities, starting in the mid-1950s, which saw thousands of Indigenous children taken from their homes and families, placed in foster homes, and eventually adopted out to white families from across Canada and the United States. These children lost their names, languages, and a connection to their heritage. Sadly, many were also abused and made to feel ashamed of who they are.

I immigrated to Canada in the last two decades. My experience tells me that although a lot of work has been done and is still in the works to address the past and present wrongs that the Indigenous people have suffered, there is a lot of ignorance in our communities. Several years ago, when I made my first visit to Alberta from Montreal, I took a flight into Calgary and then a shuttle from the Calgary airport, heading to Canmore to visit a friend who worked in that beautiful small town tucked in the Rocky Mountains. As the shuttle left the city of Calgary, heading toward the mountains, I was fascinated to see some home structures in the "bush," similar to what I was accustomed to in my village in Zimbabwe. I am not shy, so I turned to the gentleman who sat next to me in the shuttle, and asked, "Who lives in those houses in the bush? They remind me of Africa." The gentleman put his book down, turned toward me and said in a very stern voice, "Those are the native people, very dangerous people. You do not want to mess around with them. They could shoot you." Seeing the fear in my eyes, he asked me where I was going, and I told him I was going to Canmore. Then he told me to be careful when travelling between Canmore and Calgary as there are a few reserves between these two cities. So, I got this narrative and introduction from a Caucasian Canadian about the Indigenous people. I would like to think that this was over ten years ago, and that people are less ignorant now—but no. Recently, while in an office I worked in, the news came that remains of Indigenous children were found in a mass grave in

Kamloops. Again, not being shy to discuss current affairs, I asked people in the office what their thoughts and reactions were; and to my horror, one of them responded by saying, "It's high time that those people get over it."

The residential schools savoured the relationship between parents and children and destroyed the language and culture but did not take the Indian out of the children. I cannot imagine anything taking the Zimbabwean out of me as that will be stripping me of my dignity and identity.

The UN Declaration on the Rights of Indigenous Peoples has the following key statements;

- Affirming that Indigenous peoples are equal to all other peoples while recognizing the right of all peoples to be different, to consider themselves further, and to be respected as such;
- Affirming also that all peoples contribute to the diversity and richness of civilizations and cultures, which constitute the common heritage of humankind;
- Reaffirming that Indigenous peoples, in the exercise of their rights, should be free from discrimination of any kind;
- Concerned that Indigenous peoples have suffered from historic injustices as a result of, among other things, their colonization and dispossession of their lands, territories and resources, thus preventing them from exercising, in particular, their right to development by their own needs and interests;

Emphasizing the contribution of the demilitarization of the lands and territories of Indigenous peoples to peace, economic and social progressed development, understanding and friendly relations among nations and peoples of the world.

In Canada, the Truth and Reconciliation Commission (TRC) report resulted from a 6-year-long inquiry undertaken by the TRC into the legacy of the Residential School System. The Commission was established in 2006 as part of a class action settlement agreement between the Government of Canada, the churches responsible for running the Residential School System, and the survivors of the system. The settlement agreement resulted from a process led by survivors of the Residential School System, working over decades. The Commission's mandate included promoting awareness of the Residential School System and its impacts, creating a historical record of the system and its legacy, and recommending changes across Canadian society to further the process of reconciliation.

The Residential School System was a system of boarding schools for Aboriginal children, established by the government and administered by several Christian churches. The schools began as a government policy in the early 1800s, and were authorized by statute, by Canada, upon confederation. The TRC found that, for much of its operational history, the policy underlying the Residential School System was an attempt at cultural genocide, to systematically assimilate Indigenous peoples by forcibly separating children from their families and suppressing Indigenous languages and traditions and other cultural elements (as noted in the TRC's final report). There is a growing recognition in Canada, across all sectors and regions, of the need for a deeper understanding and more meaningful inclusion of the Indigenous people of Canada. One of the centrepieces of this recognition was the final report of the Truth and Reconciliation Commission of Canada, released in 2015, which included 94 calls to action to effect reconciliation with Indigenous peoples.

LBGTQ

I was raised Catholic; I grew up in a patriarchal society, and in that society, it was, and is, still "illegal" to be gay or lesbian. My subconscious was trained to protect myself from anyone of a different sexual orientation. No homosexual people. So, I was homophobic. You can imagine the shock to my belief system when I moved to Canada twenty years ago and discovered that it was acceptable to have a different sexual orientation. I had told myself that I would protect myself by staying away from anyone who professed to be gay or lesbian. I did not know about bisexual, transgender, or other descriptions.

One of my colleagues that I worked with at the Fairmont Banff Springs saved me. His name is Mark, and I have been looking for him to thank him for helping me overcome my fear and bias toward anyone of a different sexual orientation. This is how it happened. Mark was a hard-working gentleman. He seemed very comfortable with himself and accepted other people who were non-Caucasian. I thought that he was a good man, maybe a Christian. So, I decided whenever I had a question about work or how to deal with a colleague or an employee, I would go to Mark, and I did. Each time, he would stop whatever he was doing, be present, listen to me and usually ask my thoughts before he jumped into giving me his advice. I really started to respect Mark and had this trusting relationship with him. We were colleague supervisors, and I began to look up to him as a mentor. My learning moment took place at a Christmas dinner where managers and supervisors celebrated in the Italian restaurant that was part of the hotel. People brought their spouses, and we introduced them to the team. Mark introduced a man that sat next to him as his spouse. I almost fell off my chair. It was at that moment that I realized how biases can cripple us. I would have had any other man at the table professing to be gay, but not Mark; yet, I liked and respected Mark. It was a moment of recognizing that lesbians and gays, or whatever label we put on people with different sexual orientations, are also human. So, I made that journey to seek out people of other sexual orientations and have a curious conversation about their experiences. I found out that much of what I struggled with being discriminated against, they faced it too.

I have learnt a lot in twenty years. I now have friends in the LBGTQ+ community. I am sharing this story to show you that we all have biases and can unlearn the false beliefs we acquire on our journey. But here is the challenge: You cannot accept what you have not taken the time to get to know or befriend. For that reason, I decided to share some helpful terms that you can use as a starting point to understand fellow humans who are in the LBGTQ community. I have listened to different members of this community, and the one common thread I have heard them say loud and clear is, "Treat me as human."

Canada has made significant strides toward celebrating and protecting LGBTQ2S+ PEOPLE AND THEIR FAMILIES. Gender identity and gender expression were added as protected grounds against discrimination, in *Canada's Human Rights Act*, in 2017.

Sexual Orientation

This describes a person's emotional and/or sexual attraction to others. For many, sexual orientations can be fluid and may change over time. I had to unlearn that there is only one sexual orientation—a man is attracted to a woman and vice versa—and that this is determined by your sex when you are born and will not change until you die.

Gender Expression

This is the external and public presentation of a person's gender, expressed through one's name, pronouns, clothing, hair, behaviour, voice, or other body characteristics. Social norms identify these as masculine and feminine traits. However, traditionally, our societies have had two gender categories for gender identity. You will notice that birth certificates, national identification documents (ID) and voter registries typically have space for male or female self-identification boxes. However, these are changing slowly, with progressive communities adding other categories.

When I was at the University of Zimbabwe between 1998 and 2001, we had a professor who was gay. He was also the former vice president of the country. His name was Canaan Banana. He was a professor of liberation theology. Each time he came to campus to teach, students ridiculed him and hailed insults at him. While I did not participate in the abuses, I never said anything. I did not speak up and tell my colleagues that it was wrong. One of the lessons that I have learned in this work is to stand up and speak up when I see bias and discrimination.

As this book is on inclusion, I wanted to share some inclusive languages you can learn and use for the LGBTQ2S+ community. Inclusive language challenges us to tap into our conscious minds and avoid assumptions. For example, I have learned to share my pronouns when introducing myself. When you meet a person, you ask the name they go by and their pronoun. Asking shows you respect the person and do not want to assume.

Our names are important to all of us regardless of our gender. For example, my name is Ntombizodwa, a Ndebele expression that literally means "only girls." This is part of my identity, story, and history. When I was born, I was the sixth girl born in our family. The name is a description of the family situation at that time. I often joke with my parents that they complained that they had too many girls, and then the long-awaited boy came after me. Now, the importance of a name is the same for gender-diverse people. When we use the name that they go by, we tell them that we respect and care about who they are, and that they are accepted for who they are.

Using inclusive language will go a long way in creating a sense of belonging for everyone, including gender-diverse people. I often see it in children when we assume they have both a dad and a mom, and how damaging it can be for a child who is from a single-parent home. Similarly, when we assume that all parents are male and female, if there is a child from a gay couple or a lesbian couple, that automatically makes them feel different and not like other kids. For example, I watched *Modern Family*, a sitcom and mockumentary. In this sitcom, a gay couple adopts a little Asian girl. There are many funny episodes, and I found a lot of lessons about how our world is changing fast.

Here are some inclusive words you can use today to stand out as an inclusive leader in your job or community.

Instead of:	Use:
Chairman	Chairperson
Husband or wife	Spouse
Mother or father	Parent
Boyfriend or girlfriend	Partner
Postman	Post
He/she	They

One of the considerations for inclusivity is creating a safe space for people of gender diversity. If a person discloses their sexual orientation or gender identity to you, they have shared something very personal that requires trust and confidentiality. Unless the person says I would like you to share this with the team, you have no right to share that information. Sharing information about an individual's sexual orientation or gender identity that is not known by others, is referred to as "outing." Outing can damage the relationship, cause a loss of trust, and expose the person to a significant risk of discrimination.

Combatting Discrimination Against People With Disabilities

In my teens, I was exposed to the children who were deaf and dumb at Emerald Hill School for the Deaf, run by the Dominican Missionary sisters in Harare, Zimbabwe. It was the first time I realized I was privileged to speak and hear. I learnt sign language to communicate with these children. In my class at the Dominican Convent High School, I had a classmate who was blind, and she used brail for her books and writing. I share these stories to show you that it is difficult to imagine the struggles of certain groups in our communities, unless we are exposed to them or intentionally seek them out to understand them.

Most countries have laws that make discrimination against people with disabilities illegal. The gap is in enforcement. In other areas, the gap is a lack of awareness; people do not know their rights and how to claim them. According to the UN handbook, *From Exclusion to Equality: Realizing the Rights of Persons with Disabilities*, 20% of the world's poorest people have disabilities; 98% of children with disabilities in developing countries do not attend school; around a third of the world's street children live with disabilities; and the literacy rate for adults with disabilities is as low as 3%, and 1% for women with disabilities in some countries.

Persons with disabilities are among the most marginalized in any crisis-affected community. An estimated **9.7 million persons with**

disabilities are forcibly displaced due to persecution, conflict, violence, and other human rights violations. In some cases, the morbidity of persons with disabilities in a disaster has been estimated at a rate of **4 times higher than those without disabilities.**

The principles proclaimed in the Charter of the United Nations recognize the inherent dignity and worth and the equal and inalienable rights of all human family members as the foundation of freedom, justice and peace in the world;

Reaffirming the universality, indivisibility, interdependence and interrelatedness of all human rights and fundamental freedoms, and the need for persons with disabilities to be guaranteed their full enjoyment without discrimination;

Concerned about the difficult conditions faced by persons with disabilities, who are subject to multiple or aggravated forms of discrimination based on race; colour; sex; language; religion; political or other opinions; national, ethnic, Indigenous or social origin; property; birth, age or another status;

Highlighting the fact that the majority of persons with disabilities live in conditions of poverty, and in this regard recognizing the critical need to address the negative impact of poverty on persons with disabilities; Recognizing the importance of accessibility to the physical, social, economic, and cultural environment, to health and education and to information and communication, in enabling persons with disabilities to fully enjoy all human rights and fundamental freedoms.

When I worked in health care, I visited residents in our long-term care facilities, and I have not forgotten what Mary, one of the clients, said to me. She shared that one of her frustrations was using a wheelchair around the facility. Often, staff and people would come and lean on her chair or talk above her with others while she sat in the chair. It became apparent that the wheelchair, while a mode of mobility for Mary, was part of her personal space and needed to be respected.

I also spoke to one elderly gentleman who expressed his frustration with people who shout when they talk to him. The assumption is that all elderly people are hard of hearing, so one needs to increase the volume when talking to them.

Mindfulness

What is your organization/community doing to accommodate people with disabilities?

What was your "aha" moment of this group?

What action will you take to be more inclusive of people with disabilities today?

CHAPTER SIX

The Human Heart
– Why a Sense of Belonging Is Key

"I have a dream that my four little children will one day live in a nation where they will not be judged by the colour of their skin but by the content of their character."
– Martin Luther King, Jr.

Self-actualization
desire to become the most that one can be

Esteem
respect, self-esteem, status, recognition, strength, freedom

Love and belonging
friendship, intimacy, family, sense of connection

Safety needs
personal security, employment, resources, health, property

Physiological needs
air, water, food, shelter, sleep, clothing, reproduction

Maslow's hierarchy of needs

The experience of COVID-19 and the subsequent effects of the Russian war on Ukraine, and a looming recession, has renewed attention to the concepts of inclusion and belonging as universal human needs. Social belonging is a fundamental human need hardwired into our DNA, yet 40% of people say they feel isolated at work. The Harvard Review embarked on research on the meaning of belonging, and observed that "data showed that belonging is a close cousin to many related experiences: mattering, identification and social connection. The unifying thread across these themes is that they all revolve around the sense of being accepted and included by those around you."

Similar studies have shown that companies reap substantial bottom-line benefits if workers feel like they belong. High belonging was linked to a whopping 56% increase in job performance, a 50% drop in turnover risk and a 75% reduction in sick days. For a 10,000-person company, this would result in annual savings of more than $52M. Employees with higher workplace belonging also showed a 167% increase in their employer promoter score (their willingness to recommend their company to others). They also received double the raises and 18 times more promotions.

Increasingly, the word that crops up when we talk about workplace communities is "belonging." Psychologist Abraham Maslow identified the importance of belonging, 80 years ago, positioning it just above the need for safety; and today, other researchers have moved it up the ranks, saying it's as necessary as food and shelter.

Why? Because it's human nature to crave community, and the connection is a basic human need. In a somewhat less-defined form, this idea has now moved into the lexicon of diversity, equity, and inclusion. The pandemic amplified the concept when forced isolation left many craving connection and community. It was as if we only now discovered that belonging is essential for our well-being.

Janet M. Stovall discusses the definition of belonging and says that despite its growing popularity, belonging is elusive and often feels unattainable. Why belonging is so hard to get right is quite simple: It's complicated, both in concept and execution.

In her book, *Belonging: Remembering Ourselves Home,* Toko-pa Turner makes this profound statement on belonging: We live in one of the most connected times on Earth, but never have we been so lonely, so alienated from each other, from ourselves and from the natural world. Whether this manifests as having difficulty finding community, feeling anxiety about your worthiness and place in the world, or simply feeling disconnected, the absence of belonging is the great silent wound of our times. Most of us think of belonging as a place outside of ourselves that, if we keep searching, maybe one day we'll find. But what if belonging isn't a place but a set of skills or competencies that we in modern times have lost or forgotten." Studies have shown that children who have not achieved a healthy attachment in their young lives have lower self-esteem, a more pessimistic worldview, are mistrustful and can have a perception of rejection. Belonging is a fundamental part of being human; we need people, and this need is hardwired into our brains.

Depression, anxiety and suicide are common mental health conditions associated with lacking a sense of belonging. These conditions can lead to social behaviour that interferes with a person's ability to connect to others, creating a cycle of events that further weakens a sense of belonging. On the other hand, a sense of belonging can be so powerful that it can create both value in life and the ability to learn healthy coping skills when experiencing intensive and painful emotions. According to research, an individual's well-being can be jeopardized by only one instance of exclusion. That is powerful when I think of how many instances of exclusion most people experience daily.

Humans have an instinctive need to belong. Evolutionarily, cooperation and group relationships led to an increased level of survival. So, Maslow felt it was essential to place belongingness above physiological and safety needs in his hierarchy of needs. Since the dawn of our species, there have been "containers" belonging to families, tribes, countries, and religions, to name a few. But in the modern age, all of these are changing—breaking down perhaps—widening and becoming less distinct.

The need to belong includes romantic relationships and ties to friends and family members. It also has our need to feel that we belong to a social group. Importantly, this need encompasses both feeling loved and feeling love toward others. Our intrinsic need to belong drives us to form relationships with other people. It also motivates us to create and belong to groups with like-minded people, like religious groups, clubs, sports teams, professional groups, friendship teams and others.

Belonging is a fundamental part of being human: We need people, and this need is hardwired into our DNA. A recent MIT study found that we crave interactions in the same region of our brains where we crave food. Another study showed we experience social exclusion in the same part of our brain where we experience physical pain.

Our brains use similar circuits to handle physical and social pain and pleasure. Therefore, social pains can be felt as keenly as physical injuries. When someone is excluded, isolated or feels they don't belong, it is, quite literally, painful. Belonging, however, stimulates the social pleasure circuits and can alleviate that pain or not cause it in the first place. A lack of belonging can also cause stress, depression, and anxiety. These can initiate a vicious cycle of self-destructive behaviours that further prevent a person from belonging.

The University of British Columbia found that when we experience ostracism at work, it can lead to job dissatisfaction and health problems. Similarly, a study at the University of Michigan found that when people lack a sense of belonging, it is a strong predictor of depression. In fact, it is an even stronger predictor than feelings of loneliness or a lack of social support. A strong sense of belonging is good for employees' mental and physical health. Employees who feel they belong, take 75% fewer sick days than those who feel excluded.

Belonging is necessary for our performance—individually, in teams and for our organizations—because we can more effectively engage and bring our best selves to work. And even more importantly, belonging is good for our well-being as humans. It's essential for individual physical, mental and emotional health, and it's critical to the health of our communities. The pandemic has brought belonging into sharpened focus, and our opportunity is to find a way to create it for ourselves and others. While our understanding of belonging continues to evolve, we know it is a crucial component of inclusion. It has often been proven to have excellent outcomes for employees and businesses. These last few years have repeatedly reminded us of the importance of focusing on diversity, equity, and inclusion (DEI) in the workplace, and growing expectations from employees that this will be an operational imperative in the companies they want to work for.

In her book, *Braving the Wilderness: The Quest for True Belonging and the Courage to Stand Alone*, Brené Brown says, "I don't think there's anything lonelier than being with people and feeling alone." I can't tell you how often I've been surrounded by people and felt utterly alone. It's hands down one of the worst feelings, because the logical part of you is screaming, "How could you possibly feel alone right now? There are so many people to talk to!" But your heart is saying, "But I don't want to talk to anyone. No one understands me here." In my job as a family and divorce lawyer, I have met many people who have talked about the lonely feelings that haunted them in their marriages.

I have been there, too, in a crowd and alone. I have felt that I do not belong, many times. It shakes the core of who you are as a human being. I lost confidence, and when the confidence was lost, I was ineffective. I could not perform at the level I used to know of myself. I have often asked this question: "What is the hardest transition for you, moving from Zimbabwe to Canada?" I can tell you that it is feeling that I do not belong, that I am an outsider. I have often reflected on why this has been one of the deepest struggles, and I have thought of a few possible answers to this. First, I come from a society where the community has priority over individuality. Second, I come from a big family of 8 siblings and have always belonged to different groups.

Moving to a new country and continent and starting life anew was the direct opposite of what I had known all my life. Third, I began understanding some of the health conditions I associated with the Western world. Back in Zimbabwe, I had not heard of health issues like anxiety, depression, or panic attacks. Social disconnection has become a concerning trend across many developed cultures for several reasons, including social mobility, technological shifts, broken families and community structures, and the pace of modern life (Baumeister & Robson, 2021). The COVID-19 pandemic magnified and accelerated the struggles that already existed. Early studies investigating the social and mental health impacts of the pandemic have pointed to increases in loneliness and mental illness, especially among vulnerable populations, that are caused at least in part by extended periods of isolation, social distancing, and rising distrust of others.

Although belonging occurs as a subjective feeling, it exists within a dynamic social milieu. Biological needs complement, accentuate and interact with social structures, norms, contexts, and experiences (Slavich, 2020). Social, cultural, environmental, and geographical structures, broadly defined, provide an orientation for the self to determine who and what is acceptable, the nature of right and wrong, and a sense of belonging or alienation (Allen, 2020b). Deloitte defines a worker's sense of belonging as how organizations can foster diverse, equitable and inclusive communities for the worker and how they feel like a member of the broader world. This impacts how employees show up and feel comfortable being themselves and contribute to an organization's common goals.

According to Deloitte research, creating a sense of belonging requires three mutually reinforcing attributes:

Comfort: Individuals feel comfortable at work, including being treated fairly and respected by their colleagues and leaders.

"I am valued for who I am, my background and my beliefs. So, I can bring my authentic self to work."

Connection: Individuals feel they have meaningful relationships with coworkers and teams and are connected to the organization's goals.
"I am a part of something larger than myself. I provide support and am supported by my workplace community."

Contribution: Individuals feel that they contribute to meaningful outcomes, understanding how their strengths help to achieve common goals.

"I (we) add value by bringing unique skills and strengths to meaningfully contribute to shared purposes and goals."

One thing is clear: Employees want to feel a sense of belonging at work, and everybody must be brave to make this happen. But ticking the boxes isn't enough either; sometimes companies need to remember that even if someone is **included**, it doesn't necessarily mean they feel they **belong**. And belonging *is* a feeling—a much more formidable force than any DEI strategy handbook can offer. As Anita Sands puts it: *"Diversity is a **fact** (the numbers are what they are), inclusion is a **choice** (you decide whether to include someone or not),* *but belonging is a **feeling** that can be enforced by a culture you can purposefully create."*

I decided to put belonging at the centre of this book because science and experience have shown us that there has been a lot of focus on diversity, equity, and inclusion, yet much has not been accomplished. People need to be accepted for who they are to feel they belong. Safe spaces must be created. Amy Edmondson, the premier expert on psychological safety, defines it as "a belief that one will not be punished or humiliated for speaking up with ideas, questions, concerns or mistakes." Often misunderstood as being comfortable or agreeable, psychological safety is present when employees feel they're part of an environment where challenge, conflict and mistakes are valued, and learning is a team sport. Hallmarks of a psychologically safe environment are seen when individuals can take risks, experiment, and fail, without fear of repercussions.

Psychological safety isn't the absence of things going wrong but rather the absence of the fear of negative consequences *when* things go wrong. Things will go wrong—that's just life. To overcome the natural tendency to stay silent and avoid conflict, team members and leaders need to provide support, not comfort. Edmondson observed at the beginning of her journey: Many lives are at stake when individuals cannot speak up. "It will always be safer to hold back than to jump in," she says. "In today's work environment, that can prove catastrophic and counterproductive. That's created a greater need for psychological safety as things are more uncertain and fast-moving. We depend more on each other, and we may be at risk of not hearing from each other."

CHAPTER SEVEN

Inclusive Leadership

"Everything rises and falls on leadership."
– John C. Maxwell

G reater team diversity does not automatically yield an inclusive climate (Tanachia Ashkali, "The Role of Inclusive Leadership in Supporting an Inclusive Environment in Diverse Public Sector Teams"). Research has shown that more than simply enhancing the representation of more diverse employees is required. To fully tap into the intended outcomes of diversity, organizations need to focus on including those are historically marginalized. (MOR Barak Et Al., 2016, Shore et al., 2018).

Drawing on optimal distinctiveness theory, inclusion has been conceptualized as dependent on two needs that individuals seek to satisfy: belongingness and uniqueness. (Shore et al. I, 2011). A sense of belonging involves individuals seeking similarities and validation from others. Uniqueness refers to individuals seeking individuality in comparison with others. Seeking similarities is evident in many conversations. For example, when I mention that I am from Zimbabwe, most people would respond by saying that they have met or worked with a Zimbabwean or travelled to the country, validating the need to find common ground. To experience inclusion, individuals need to feel they belong to the group, meaning that each member is treated as an insider while having the opportunity to sustain and express their unique identities. This requires differences among team members to be valued. Everyone is encouraged to remain authentic rather than being assimulated by the dominant groups.

An example is the colonization process. France used the process of assimilation. The Cambridge Advanced Learner's Dictionary defines assimilation as becoming like others by taking in and using their customs and culture. The difference is that in the colonization context, assimilation was not a choice, but something forced onto communities and countries. In Canada, we have an example of a forced assimilation process on Indigenous people through the creation of the residential schools, whose goal was to "take the Indian out of the Indigenous children." Such an approach has resulted in transgenerational trauma and damage, and the effects of the harm will take generations to repair. While the example of residential schools is profound, the reality of what marginalized groups experience daily when they mask to fit in and be accepted is significant. For example, many organizations use the term "culture fit" for hire. Such messaging supports discriminatory workplace practices and stunts progress in creating diverse teams.

Inclusive leaders are open to differences and respect differences and want to learn more. Inclusive leaders are those that inspire others but also let themselves be inspired by others. Expressed differently, inclusive leaders have a growth mindset, where they have moved from a "know-it-all mindset" to "learn it all." They lead from behind, observing each individual and innovating on how they can continuously flourish talent or support others in growing their talent.

Finally, inclusive leaders are the ones that are going to value you, respect you and help you during your time in the company. From a very human perspective, many people crave to be seen and loved for the very thing that makes them unique. When a leader can see an individual for who they are first, before looking for what they can contribute, they create a sense of belonging. In my legal practice, when I do the first intake interview with a client, I must practice the process of creating a space to see the person first before defining them in their problem; and a hundred percent of the time, the client has said: "I trust you and believe my case is in good hands." Most of the clients have been going through a dark moment; for some, they are going through a painful separation and divorce, and for others, it's challenges with their immigration application or human rights issues. Creating a safe space and validating that the individual matters is the first step in demonstrating leadership. Here is the thing: leadership is a journey not a destination; it took me twenty years of learning and development to be a good leader, and I am still learning as I want to move from a good to a great leader.

I remember my green years as a leader. One example that comes to mind is when I became a teacher and program manager at a high school in Harare, in 2001. Before I completed my bachelor's degree, my high school principal asked me if I could take a teaching position at my former school. This was a fascinating and challenging offer, and exciting in that this was a prestigious school in the country. In other words, it was an honour for me! It was also a challenge in that I had to now work with my former teachers as my colleagues. The challenge was that the principal wanted me to bring back interest in the subject of history, as most students did not like the subject, and their performance in exams was poor. As a rookie teacher with no experience, I was tasked to be head of the history department.

My first learning was that I did not know much about leadership, teaching, and management. I needed to be open to learning. My principal was very supportive and a great mentor. I felt uncomfortable my first time facilitating a meeting as I had senior teachers who had taught for years in my department. I decided to assure everyone on my team that I valued their experience and knowledge, and as a team, we would work together to bring the interest in history subject back. I survived my first meeting. After all, the attitude was not as bad as I anticipated! To make my story short, at the end of my second year at St. Dominic's high school, history was a popular subject. The school was on national TV twice, showcasing creative ways of learning history and great Cambridge A-level results.

Looking back, I learned the following about leadership and management:

A leader needs to be **human**, believing in people, giving them the benefit of the doubt, and empowering them to do what is in their power to do their best. This means recognizing that people have lives outside work and can make mistakes, which is okay.

As a leader, I learnt **honesty and fairness**; when those I lead do a good job, I acknowledge it timely. Likewise, I recognize their strengths and let them know. Similarly, I let them know respectfully and firmly when they are wrong.

I learnt that consistency in **performance management** is vital for productivity, coaching and learning with fairness and honesty.

Above all, and among other lessons, I learnt that being a great leader and manager begins with self. If I am at home with who I am, I will understand that **leadership is not about power. It is about positive influence.**

One of the best tools in our arsenal as leaders is storytelling. Using the analogy of an iceberg, storytelling helps to dive deeper, below the 10% of what we see above the sea, and it gives us a sneak peek into the 90%. The storyteller lets you into their sacred space, and you need to suspend judgment, lean in and experience the teaching moment. It creates a bond that is built on trust and shared experiences. It enhances a safe space and a feeling of acceptance. It cuts into the core of who we are as humans. Leaders need to listen deeply to the people. As a leader, you can use storytelling as a powerful tool to bring to life real-lived experiences.

In the wake of the murder of George Floyd, on May 25, 2020, as a black person, I was triggered by the whole event, and some of my own lived experiences of racism bubbled up. I did not know who to talk to or share with, so I wrote a letter to the organization's vice president.

Now you need to understand that I worked for a large organization with over a hundred thousand people; writing to the VP was like writing to the leader of a country. I share this experience because I was pleasantly surprised by the leadership demonstrated by this man. The letter was quite direct; I used facts and shared my perspective, and I was expecting to be punished or admonished or something negative. The response I got was an invitation for a discussion, so I spent days putting together my "defence," coming from my typical lawyer mind. What the VP did at the beginning of our meeting helped me let my guard down and feel safe, and I learnt from him. To quote him verbatim, here is how he opened the meeting… "Thank you for reaching out and sending me a letter. I must acknowledge that it was not easy to read it. I had to sleep over it. After reflecting on what you said, I felt it was a great opportunity for us to talk, so I am here to listen and learn." Wow, that was the incredible experience of my 15 years working for that organization. I can tell you that I have received numerous job offers from other organizations, but I have stayed with my current organization because someone took the brave, inclusive step to say to me that they see me and value me for who I am.

Minorities in the workplace spend over 50% of their time masking. Masking refers to hiding your authentic self to gain greater social acceptance. The costs of camouflaging your true personality and emotions can add up exponentially, causing one to experience a sense of loss, anxiety, and depression. I have been there. I spent more of my work life thinking about how to fit in. My colleagues would make facial expressions when I pronounced a word differently, or sometimes they would laugh so much that I got confused about whether they were laughing with me or at me. I remember the many times I had to force myself to eat food I did not want to eat because I wanted to fit in.

When I moved to Canada, I did not drink coffee or alcohol. I slowly learnt how to drink coffee, as most of the time, that was the drink provided in our meetings. When we went for dinners, I would order juice, and my colleagues would look at me and say, "Really?" I felt the pressure to try alcohol, and I did not know the names when ordering. Imagine the emotional energy that goes with that. To add to that, English is my second language. I would translate in my head before I spoke during my first days. After 22 years, English is almost my first language, and when I go home, I translate from English to Shona. As a leader, it is crucial to keep this in mind, allow time to process, remove barriers and acknowledge that employees use different energies during their workday. Contrary to the common assumption that immigrants or those who use English as a second language are less smart, the reality is that they are more intelligent because they can access different parts of the brain to use other languages.

Your job is to listen more and talk less. One of the leadership lessons that Nelson Mandela passed on was a lesson from his father. His father taught him that one of the great leadership traits is to be the last one to speak. Listening is more challenging than talking. If you care deeply about the people under your care, you will always be intentional and ask yourself how best you can serve them. How will you be present? Listening is one of the sexiest traits of a leader. I am on a new team where meetings do not follow the agenda, and discussions are popcorn-style. I have struggled just to have my voice heard, and the people are passionate and pressed for time, so whoever is the fasted in unmuting their microphones speak. Some people also talk to think; others like to hear their voices, with no sensitivity to taking turns. A leader needs to manage a meeting platform and ensure that 20% of the members don't do 80% of the speaking during meetings.

If diversity is counting heads, and inclusion is making the heads count, it is the leader's role to ensure every head on their team counts. I have been asked how one can make sure each head counts. The answer is that it depends. Sometimes it is about inviting members who do not spontaneously speak to have their voices heard. Increased belonging reduces turnover and increases performance by 56%. Other times it is when distributing tasks and projects; team members like to put up their hand for everything. As a leader busy with multiple competing priorities, it is easy to just have the job done without doing due diligence to ensure your team's equity. Being intentional in your decisions and transparency around the rationale for those decisions is key to creating a safe space and a sense of belonging for all team members. Inclusive leaders are open to seeing different views and perspectives. This can happen when we are not defensive or judgemental.

The biggest drivers for team effectiveness are psychological safety and dependability, structure, clarity, meaning and impact. That psychological safety is essential is no surprise, as people can only bring their best selves to work when they feel they belong and are allowed to be who they are and are valued for who they are first, ahead of what they can bring to the table. In one organization where I worked, the leadership was surprised when I gave them my one-month notice to resign. There was no mention of the value I brought to the position in the conversation. There was no acknowledgement of my work ethic or team spirit, but more of what I might get down the road if I stayed. I did not feel valued for who I was but for the money I was bringing into the organization, so I decided to go to a team where I was loved for who I was first.

In another organization that I worked for; my boss would always check his Apple watch. He would walk away before I finished talking, and I often felt dismissed and unheard. I quickly learnt what kind of boss I did not want to be. I did not dare tell this man how I felt. He was a great guy and well-meaning. An active part of lifelong learning is listening. Listening does a few things to another person. First, it says, "I can see and value you and am present." Listening creates a psychologically safe space and builds trust. Listening starts with day-to-day courtesies like asking, "How are you?" When you ask the question, make sure you care to listen.

Humans have it in their DNA to want to belong, be part of the whole and be in the ingroup. We crave community. I remember when I moved from Zimbabwe to Canada, I knew that life had changed, but I was unaware of what was happening inside me. I landed at Dorval airport in Montreal, Quebec, on November 21, 2001, and I did not speak French. I had left my family, friends and community in Zimbabwe and was now in the out-group. I lost confidence. I thought something had changed in me when I crossed the ocean. I did not feel beautiful, intelligent, witty, vivacious, kind and many more traits that my friends used to define me back in Zimbabwe. For the longest time, I did not feel I belonged to anyone or a team.

The global workforce has changed, and so have customer needs. As a result, there is growing literature on inclusive leadership and its traits or qualities. But first, I will discuss the framework provided by Deloitte. Key traits of inclusive leadership by Deloitte:

Commitment

Many leaders make verbal commitments. However, they must articulate how their personal values align with diversity, equity, and inclusion. The only way a leader can align is to ask themselves why they do what they do. Self-reflection will go a long way to getting a leader grounded. Identify when the concepts of equity and inclusion became salient for you.

Courage

Once grounded and committed, courage comes from within. The fear of making mistakes dissipates because you will act from a space of acknowledging your imperfections; you will have the courage to face yourself and be humble. Courage is the conviction that you know you could be better. You will have the proper humility to accept when you say the wrong things and make mistakes. Such courage will create an ethically safe space for others to be themselves and acknowledge their imperfections; in other words, be human. You will stand in the power of what you believe to be correct and challenge the status quo. The NeuroLeadership Institute says inclusive leaders act boldly.

Curiosity

Curiosity stems from a growth mindset. It is the ability to accept that your worldview is one of many and is not the correct one but just different. Curiosity is a springboard that nudges us to seek out those different from us and be genuinely interested in getting to know them. It is the beauty of expanding ourselves by expanding our circles and connections. From a leadership perspective, it asks important questions like, who is missing at the table? What diverse perspectives can support innovation?

Collaboration

Create a safe space for team members to work together and collaborate outside the team. Allowing for the permeability and pollination of ideas will be a great way to demonstrate collaboration.

Cognizance of Bias

As mentioned under commitment, self-reflection, and the acknowledgement that we are biased if we have a brain, an inclusive leader stands out in using mitigating strategies to deal with their own bias.

Cultural Intelligence

This is how a leader can effectively navigate different cultures and perspectives, by having the ability to challenge stereotypes and systems, and the ability to demonstrate a high tolerance for ambiguity.

Korn Ferry's 5 disciplines of inclusive leadership:

Authenticity
Requires humility, setting aside ego and establishing trust in the face of opposing beliefs, values, or perspectives.

Emotional Resilience
Requires the ability to remain composed in the face of adversity and difficulty around differences.

Inquisitiveness
Requires openness to differences, curiosity and empathy.

Self-assurance
Requires a stance of confidence and optimism.

Flexibility
Requires the ability to tolerate ambiguity and to be adaptable to diverse needs.

I propose three keys to standing out as an inclusive leader. These are:

- Self-care inclusive leadership is from the inside out. It starts with recognizing and accepting the diversity within the self. It includes the ability to feel and process an uncomfortable feeling, and this has been called emotional intelligence.
- Care deeply for those in your charge.
- Take care of the business.

CHAPTER EIGHT

Creating a Space for Belonging

"Leadership is unlocking people's potential to become better."
– Bill Bradley

Simon Sinek talks about leadership as an inert, learned, and practicable skill. Everyone can be a leader, but only some people want to be a leader, and not everyone has to be a leader. When you choose to be a leader, however, you need clarity on why you accept a leadership position. Why do you want to lead? Leadership is not power or title. It is responsibility and sacrifice. As Sinek puts it, "… it is not about being in charge but taking care of those in your charge." Ken Blanchard puts it another way. He says leadership is all about the people you serve, not your ego. I will add that leadership is a way of being. To lead other people effectively, you need to lead yourself first. When one has proved they can lead themselves, they can be entrusted with leading others.

A leader's job is to make it safe for people to fail. This is about something other than the failures caused by incompetency or not following a standard protocol (when it exists). That is not the kind of failure a leader should tolerate. On the other hand, failure should not only be tolerated and accepted when there is a need to experiment and try new things. It should be celebrated! It is also OK to know only some of the answers! It is OK to experiment! And it is OK to fail! Or else there may be no change, growth, or innovation. A leader's job is to invite opinions and ideas from everyone, especially the silent team members. Inclusive leadership ensures that all voices are heard. When everyone on the team agrees with the leader without having any thoughts, it is a sign that your team might lack psychological safety. When team members no longer voice their opinions, they might have checked out. I recently talked with a friend who had just celebrated their tenth work anniversary. I asked them how they felt, and they responded that they were now on the job for the paycheck. When I asked them to say more about their response, they said, "I attend meetings and never contribute, and I do not share my ideas anymore, because when I did, I was never heard."

Research forecasts that in 2030, women will make up 51% of the workforce, we will continue to have 5 generations in the workplace, people of colour will make up over 50% of the USA population, and 40% will work remotely and part-time. The workforce will continue to shift dramatically in a wide variety of complexes. Organizations and leaders will need to brand themselves to attract top talent. To attract and retain talent, leaders must develop the muscle for inclusion, and true inclusion is when people feel they belong. A leader sets direction and creates an environment where team members can flourish.

Research has demonstrated numerous ways that people leave bad bosses and toxic environments. John Maxwell says that everything rises and falls on leadership. Leaders have a direct impact on the employee. The challenge is that today's leadership is challenged as things change rapidly.

Recognize that the old way of working at the office has changed. Gone are the days when you could walk into the office and employees run to their desks and get to work. While it sounds funny and more like a scene in a movie, it is true. My sister, who lives in the United States, got a management position at a young age. In her green years, she wore high heels and would make a statement when getting to the office, so that people would know the boss was coming. You can no longer walk into the building and see your employees and assure yourself that everyone showed up and on time and is healthy and busy with organizational work and not shopping on Amazon.

Many leaders are feeling a loss of control and anxiety around trust. Data has shown that for some companies, productivity went down. The key is to focus on the work's output and quality of the work, and not the inputs. One of the components of building trust is giving people autonomy. Giving autonomy is one of the biggest fears for leaders. They feel that giving people freedom means losing control. It feels like losing the ability to direct employees to the results required by the organization. Some leaders have adopted a surveillance approach that makes them think they have regained control. Leaders need to adopt a growth mindset. Neuroscience has shown us that our brains can grow if we are open to learning and changing our habits.

Pat Wadors says there is a significant correlation between a sense of belonging and engagement and performance. People will take less pay and lower titles to do their best work. Gallup research shows that 20%

of the people at the table speak 80% of the time. So how do you, as a leader, facilitate meetings? Inclusive meetings ensure all voices are heard and acknowledged.

Work is changing dramatically. We continue to experience changes seen in distributed, digital, and technology-based work. To succeed in these changing environments, a leader needs to embrace reality, care about the human beings in their charge at an individual level and create an equitable system that removes barriers for marginalized groups and employees. A leader needs to employ current trends and practices like design thinking and inclusive design. In addition, a leader must think with empathy and act with compassion.

We are expecting a lot from leaders; their jobs have changed, and we want them to be superhumans. However, everyone is going through unprecedented change and transformation. Based on their study of more than 200 organizations, and review of existing academic research, Gallup has identified three requirements for creating inclusive environments for all employees. According to Gallup, here's what an inclusive work culture looks like:

1. **Everyone treats everyone else with respect.**
   Building an inclusive culture is the shared responsibility of employees, managers, and organizational leaders. It takes intention at *every* level to sustain an inclusive workplace.

2. **Employees are valued for their strengths.**
   When employees understand their strengths, they can tap into what motivates them and what they naturally do best. They can also identify blind spots for observing, evaluating or demon-

strating respect for others.

3. **Leaders do what's right.**

    Leaders need to be fair and unbiased in hiring, assigning work, evaluating compensations, and making promotions—and hold managers accountable for doing the same.

Self-Care

Prioritize yourself, take care of yourself and choose YOU. How do you do that? Balance your basic needs of sleep, exercise, nutrition, and hydration with your leadership development. Again, there is a strong correlation between well-being and performance.

Airlines have taught us about self-care in their safety videos when they reference that if the air quality changes, oxygen masks will drop, and if you have someone in your care, you put the mask on yourself first, and then put the mask on those in your care. This shows that we cannot care for others unless we are fit. In my 20 years of experience in leadership development, I have seen and studied many leadership development frameworks and theories, and some frameworks have passed the test of time. I see value in the LEADS framework developed by Royal Roads. Leads is an acronym that stands for the following:

- Lead self
- Engage others
- Achieve results
- Develop coalitions
- Systems thinking

The merit of this framework is that practical, relevant, and inclusive leadership starts with the self. So, fill your cup to add value to others. You cannot give what you do not have. As Warren R. Austin puts it, "... if you would lift me, you must be on higher ground." The ability to lead yourself includes self-awareness of your strengths and limitations, your own emotions, and the ability to self-regulate those emotions. In addition, have an inclusive mindset to have constructive discomfort, recognize your fears and have the courage and humility to be vulnerable.

A leader must make that long journey connecting the heart and mind. Practice humility and act boldly. Transcend the fear of saying the wrong things, lean into the discomfort and understand that silence is no longer an option. Instead, trust with curiosity, care, and compassion. Be comfortable in having uncomfortable conversations. Be able to admit that you are not an expert. Yet, you are open to learning and grant permission to be corrected.

A leader needs to be strong, agile, and curious. The agility of thought and mindset enables you to intentionally seek diverse perspectives and strive for progress, not perfection. Leadership is about growth—for yourself, your relationships, productivity, and people. To lead well, you must embrace your need for continual improvement.

"People don't care how much you know until they know how much you care." In addition, Maxwell says, "You develop credibility with people when you connect with them and show that you genuinely care and want to help them."

Only secure leaders give power to others.

Genuine Care For Those in Your Charge

Empathy has been a buzzword in recent literature about leadership and inclusion. However, one must listen and seek understanding to feel and practice empathy. I will add that compassion is what moves one from empathy to action. Leaders must be compassionate to themselves first. Being aware that they are not perfect and leaning into the growth mindset of progress, not perfection, will go a long way in preparing you as a leader to be compassionate with others. Genuine care for those in your team means that you accept them for their humanness and that they will have both strengths and weaknesses and are not perfect. They are not cogs in a wheel but people having a human experience in the workspace.

The unique challenges and opportunities presented by COVID-19 saw the social lives and community spaces shifting. The shift and disruptions impacted the mental health and well-being of many, if not all, of us. The rise in mental health issues has shown us that our deep need to belong is at the core of being human. The value of our social bonds and containers that provide a sense of belonging is essential for understanding how we work as humans. There is no such thing as separating our work life from our personal life or achieving what we traditionally call work-life balance. While we always knew that belonging is a universal human need, we have learnt that greater social connectedness is critical for our mental well-being and performance at work.

As an inclusive leader, you must know your team and understand the unspoken team norms. In one project about belonging in the workplace, one of the participants shares the following statement, which is relatable to many: "I get paid well to do something I enjoy, and I am surrounded by clever, funny, like-minded people. And for 45 or 50 hours every week, I feel isolated." As a leader, you need to identify those who are socially excluded within your teams. You must model inclusivity in distributing tasks, running meetings, providing information, and promoting team members. Being inclusive takes courage—the courage to do the right, not the easy thing—and there is no courage without vulnerability. It is easy to hand out to those that are like us. It is easy to assign tasks to our friends and those we trust. It is easy to turn a blind eye to unacceptable behaviour. Choosing the right thing means you will be fair and honest. You will avoid favouritism; it means you will call out discriminatory conduct and have the courage to lean into the discomfort.

Care About the Business Case of the Organization

In work situations, leaders are expected to produce results. Your organization might provide services, such as health care or legal services, massage therapy or food, or you might sell products in clothing stores, food stores or drug stores. Whatever you do in your leadership position, you care about your organization. It is difficult to stand for something you do not believe in. I have talked to leaders who have shared that they took the position for the money and are not invested in the organization. My experience is that one cannot survive for long in a job they are doing only for the money. One of the criteria I use when considering a job offer is the organization's values, vision, and mission. If their values align with my personal values, it will be easier to care about the organization and to see myself reflected in the business. The mistake many leaders have made is to have the assumption that hiring a diverse workforce is enough. Research has demonstrated in many ways that diversity without inclusion won't stick. Diversity without inclusion can be tokenism. Having one person representing a religious group, another ethnic minority, and a woman to have a gender balance, is only a starting point. If diverse members are hired to check the boxes and appear diverse, it is tokenism and it sacrifices those diverse individuals.

Bringing it Together

As a leader, you need to move from traditional mindsets of "work-life balance," to integrating life and work. Achieving a balance has remained an ideal that is beyond reach. COVID-19 has shown us that we can, as humans, combine work and life. We have also learnt that leaders are workers, so we cannot lead without walking the talk. Traditionally, when most leaders were male, our world valued "busyness," spending long hours in the office and minimal time with family. There is a real risk of burnout and mental health issues, and you cannot inspire the people you lead by being a bad example. You cannot tell them to "do as I say and pay a blind eye to my actions." Drawing boundaries starts with building a solid, effective team. Having the trust that your team can get the job done, and taking yourself out of the "on-call" mindset.

Two weeks ago, I was asked to talk to emergency services leaders about self-care. I was early for the session and found the group wrapping up their morning session on operations. I conveniently sat at the back of their classroom-style setup and observed the team. I noticed a quarter of them were paying attention to two members' presentations. Some members were on their laptops, and others were on their phones, which was fascinating. I quickly thought this was a great teaching moment for my session on self-care. So, I started my session by asking if anyone was on call, and no one was on call. Then I asked a follow-up question to see if their teams were working, to which they all responded that yes, crews were on the job, and ambulances were on the road. I said, "Great; do you trust that your teams are proficient, and they do not need you?" To which they answered, "Yes." Then my following invitation was a surprise to them. I said, "Let us put our phones away, close our laptops and get ready for our session on self-care."

Long story short, the team said this was one of the best sessions they had. As a leader, I have been guilty of multitasking. Although the myth is that multitasking is required for jobs, practically, it does not serve us well because you are neither here nor there. I often do it at home when I must do the laundry, cook food, and clean the house. I have ended up burning supper or mixing colours in my laundry. Bringing it closer to work, I have registered for courses online, and while logged into a session, I am busy responding to emails. At the end of the day, I have not accomplished much as I did not learn much in the session and was not present in the emails, and I made mistakes or sent them to the wrong person, only to spend more time trying to put out the fires and fix problems. Drawing boundaries and having the ability to say no are strong skills a leader can have. To be a great leader, you do not need to demonstrate skills and abilities that are out of this world. The reality is, it is the ordinary day-to-day actions and routines we have that make us stand out as a leader.

In his book, *Developing the Leader within You 2.0*, John Maxwell quotes Pope Francis's message to church leaders about the inherent leadership diseases. He lists fifteen of them, and I chose just three that reinforce my point in this chapter. First is the disease of thinking that, as leaders, we are immortal, immune, or downright indispensable. This attitude is a sign of pride and is opposite to humility and leadership as service. You and I know at the back of our minds that we are not mortal and not indispensable. What drives the idea of indispensability is that no one can do the job better than you and that your way is the best. It is a cousin to the need to control. The second "disease" is what the Pope called excessive busyness. We live in a world that values busyness, and one must be seen as very busy. We have learnt that mindfulness and being intentional about where one spends their time and energy is the new superpower of leadership. The third "disease" is existential schizophrenia, where leaders live hypocritical double lives. I already mentioned that your influence as a leader is limited unless you walk the talk.

CHAPTER NINE

Role of the Team in
Creating an Inclusive Environment

*"Great things in business are never done by one person.
They're done by a team of people."*
– Steve Jobs

Teams need to choose inclusion as a value in their team norms. While research has consistently shown that diverse teams have a competitive advantage, the reality remains that organizations and teams can only leverage the benefits of diversity if they are truly inclusive. Diversity is having a seat at the table; inclusion is having a voice at the table; belonging is having the voice heard at the table. In practical terms, this is work that stem from the heart. Unless and until we recognize the uniqueness and value of everyone for who they are on a team, the concept of inclusion remains nebulous. Inclusion cannot be measured by how most team members think but by how everyone feels. We cannot survey the leader on how they think they are inclusive, to get a sense of the level of inclusion and belonging.

The leader's role is vital in setting the tone, and the team has a more significant role co-creating with the leader in a psychologically safe environment that fosters a sense of belonging where individuals can be their authentic selves. While writing this book, I thought hard and long for examples of when I could be my authentic self. Those examples were not coming quickly into my mind. This is because we tend to easily remember those moments when we were on the outside feeling excluded. I also realized that I was indeed my authentic self twenty years ago when I lived in Zimbabwe and was not part of a visible minority. I was energized by work and felt very creative in my job. Lately, I have used my energy to survive, and have no energy left to be my creative, energetic self.

In the recent past, I was on a team where I was made to feel that I was not in the ingroup every day—20% of the team did 80% of the talking. Whenever the leader had tasks to be distributed, she would give them to the same people, sending a clear message that some of us were not accepted, valued, and even underestimated. I was a leader at the time, and I quickly learnt what to avoid with my team. I leant that when I do not appreciate everyone's value, that shows up in more ways than intended. There is an uncommunicated message between the leader and the individual. I experienced that I was on the B or perhaps the C team for my boss. I also realized I was outside the ingroup with my colleagues. I am sure that my boss and colleagues will be surprised about how I felt, and yet the reality is that the person who is excluded suffers in silence and carries the scars.

I learnt from this personal experience that the team environment is where inclusion or exclusion is practiced. Let us consider some practical ways that you, as a team member, can help foster an inclusive environment. In the pre-covid world where work was mainly on-site, team members would go for coffee or lunch with their friends. Well, there is nothing wrong with going out with friends. In fact, Gallup says one of the strong determinants of engagement is when you have a best friend or your go-to person at work. A team that values inclusion will ensure that they reach out to other members of the team who are not their friends and invite them for coffee or lunch. We cannot appreciate people or things we do not know. To get to see a person, we need to spend intentional time with them. When we stick to our own group or friends, we deprive ourselves of diversity's richness. The complexity around respecting and valuing others is our biases. To the brain, anything different is a threat. Our subconscious is powerful, and our stereotypes significantly affect how we look at those different from us.

For a team to cultivate an inclusive environment and to create a psychologically safe space that allows people to be uniquely themselves, it requires mindfulness from every member. It can be easy for the majority in a team to be dismissive and refuse to care. Yet, much of the work done at Google and in many organizations is done collaboratively by teams. The team is the molecular unit where actual production happens, innovative ideas are conceived and tested and employees experience most of their work. But it's also where interpersonal issues, ill-suited skill sets, and unclear group goals can hinder productivity and cause friction. Team members need to care about humans at an individual level. Members need to think with empathy and act with compassion. Seek to understand marginalized humans. Overcome your fear of saying the wrong things by leaning into the discomfort. Silence is no longer an option; the only option is to speak up for what is right. Acknowledge the fact that we are all learning. Having agility of mind is one step toward overcoming bias. Finally, have the willingness to be imperfect. Perfection stunts growth. Instead, strive for progress.

Many people have asked me how we can know if a team with diverse members is inclusive. This is a good question. One of the signs is observing how meetings are conducted. In the team that I belonged to and mentioned above, our team meeting was a discussion between two members. Typically, the meeting would start with a social conversation about what was happening in the two members' lives, whether it was a restaurant experience they had or a trip they just came from. Fifteen minutes later, the boss would call the meeting to order. When the meeting finally started, there was evidence that there were prior discussions, a meeting before a meeting, and most of the time, rubber-stamping ideas were generated and discussed before the official meeting. Those outside the group realized there was no need to waste their energy bringing their best selves and best ideas. To the boss and the ingroup, we were not intelligent or high-performing individuals. In fact, in some circles, we were discussed as weak links. There are better ways to run meetings than this; this is an example of a toxic team where members are not valued.

First, the leader should run meetings in efficient and effective ways that respect both the individual's and the organization's time and money. With the new hybrid remote situation now, research shows that fewer, shorter meetings are more effective in avoiding digital fatigue for people. Data and research have consistently shown us that diverse teams reduce groupthink and uplift team intelligence. Research has also highlighted that more is needed to have diversity.

To leverage diversity as a competitive advantage, we need inclusion. Increasing diversity does not, by itself, increase effectiveness; what matters is how an organization harnesses diversity and whether it's willing to reshape its power structure.

A recent study by Google on high-performing teams found that the highest contributing factor to a high-performing team is psychological safety. As stated elsewhere, the team is the molecular unit where actual production happens, innovative ideas are conceived and tested and employees experience most of their work. But it's also where interpersonal issues, ill-suited skill sets, and unclear group goals can hinder productivity and cause friction.

Psychological Safety

Team members feel safe taking risks and being vulnerable in front of each other without fear of embarrassment, ridicule or other consequences. Psychological safety refers to an individual's perception of the consequences of taking an interpersonal risk, or a belief that a team is safe for risk-taking when seen as ignorant, incompetent, negative or disruptive. Such safety is especially important for underrepresented groups. For example, we discussed in earlier chapters how unconscious bias works. We often send unintended messages to others that they are not part of us, not as intelligent or charming or whatever stereotype we use to judge others.

In a team with high psychological safety, teammates feel safe to take risks around their team members. They feel confident that no team member will embarrass or punish anyone else for admitting a mistake, asking a question, or offering a new idea. It took me six good years to feel comfortable asking questions in the team I worked on. When I moved to Canada, I was challenged by the meaning of slang words, for example, puke. In my early days, I would go to the dictionary to look for the definition, until I realized that many were slang words local to the Canadian community. There were a lot of acronyms as well, and as many of my teammates had a nursing background, it was easy for them to talk about code pink, ECG, etc. When I reflect on those days, I marvel at how much information I missed, and no wonder I appeared slow or not so smart. I spent a lot of my energy guarding myself against embarrassment.

I have worked with teams and managers that have asked me how I would know when there is psychological safety in our team. Some of the pointers found within the Aristotle project include the following: when members feel empowered to offer their ideas and opinions, no matter how different they are from the team goals or consensus or superior's ideas. This is especially important when leveraging the diversity of thought and perspective. Another sign is when members openly admit they don't know about some things at work. It is liberating now to realize that I work for a complex organization and have lots to learn. I am usually happy to direct someone to where they can get help, and I know it's okay to say I am not sure or I don't know, or even better to say, let me find out for you. One of the most significant signs of psychological safety is when members are willing to try new things and take risks, even if it means making mistakes or failing. Willingness and the ability to try new things are what drive innovation. To have diversity improve your bottom line, team members should feel that they have each other's backs and can innovate and can admit to mistakes immediately and openly so they can be rectified.

Dependability

On dependable teams, members reliably complete quality work on time. The opposite of dependability is shirking responsibilities. I have worked with hundreds of teams, and one of the red flags I listen for when dealing with a dysfunctional and toxic team is a lack of accountability, like when team members quickly declare that specific tasks are not within their job description and that the other member dropped the ball. Work teams have a lot to learn from sports teams. I watch basketball and often marvel at how each team member must be so connected and in sync with the rest to win. I have also observed teams that buy many good players; each player is focused on their own ego, and the team does not win the championship! My favourite phrase that I give to teams as a litmus test to say when they would know that they are both a psychologically safe and high-functioning team is this: "When team members work hard to make each other look good rather than making each other look bad, then the team has reached a high functioning stage."

Structure and Clarity

Team members have clear roles, plans and goals. Every team member clearly understands job expectations. This team trait confirms what many engagement tools suggest for high-performance teams and engaged team members. Each team member should know the process of fulfilling these expectations. The consequences of the individual team member's performance are also evident. In my experience, a lack of role clarity makes for much interpersonal conflict within the team. Team processes need to be defined and followed. While it is the leader's job to set expectations and direction, it is the role of each team member to perform the duties and responsibilities for which they were hired. It is also the role of each team member to hold themselves and others accountable for the deliverable set for the team.

Meaning

Finding a sense of purpose in either the work itself or the output is essential for team effectiveness. Team members should see the value of their work. They should be able to articulate their value to the organization from a personal and team level. This should be in a short, clear statement traditionally known as the elevator speech. Now that people work remotely and only sometimes go into high-rise buildings with an elevator, it should be like a one-minute Tik Tok. Work is personally important and meaningful to the team members. The meaning of work is personal and can vary amongst many factors. These factors can be financial security, supporting family, helping the team succeed or self-expression for each individual.

Impact

Teams must feel that their work and their output are making a difference. When teams see their efforts contributing to the organization's goals, they feel their work impact. Team members believe that their work matters to the company and the customers. In law school, my goal was to pass exams, which is a reasonable and realistic goal for most students. When I was doing my articles, another word for an internship as a student lawyer, my goal was to finish in good standing and get my license. When I was licensed as an associate lawyer, the next goal was to be a partner. In all these goals, there was no connection to the original reason I wanted to be a lawyer. I wanted to help those who do not always have access to justice, and fight for human rights. I had to take a step back and reconnect my vision to my purpose. In my current job and business, the first place of evaluation to engage in work is to determine if the work will make a difference in someone's life. The leader and team members should see the impact they make in their daily work.

Ability to Navigate and Thrive in Ambiguity

A global pandemic primed us to prioritize diversity, equity and inclusion. There has been growth in the collective awareness of the need to go back to the basics of our humanness. The need for a sense of belonging is at the core of who we are as a human race. It is in our DNA as humans to form social groups and cultivate relationships. We also know that we get challenged because our brains are wired to protect us; we all have biases and most of these are unconscious. The preferences come alive when we are in crisis. It is for this reason that discrimination issues surfaced during the pandemic. As humans, we need a paradigm shift. We need to realize that what separates us is space and not differences. The distance we create between us is more in our minds and emotions. Racism is the fruit of economic domination.

Systems were put in place to protect and perpetuate domination. The plans are intact but functioning the way they were designed to work. We need to move from tokenism to realism and move from not being racist to being anti-racist. People can smell inauthenticity from a mile away. Some leaders have gained more power by promoting themselves in support of diversity. Diversity and inclusion are not about black, brown or white. It's not about who you worship, and it's not about your political affiliation; it's about human dignity. Truth must come before reconciliation. The transformational change we seek requires us to pause, be humble to learn the truth and act to dismantle biases and systems that brought us here.

The challenge with the pandemic is that we continue to be in flux, wondering if we are at the beginning, middle or end. The onset of the pandemic sent shock waves, and we lived on high adrenaline; then we got fatigued, and then we hoped that with the vaccine, we were going back to our new normal, but then another variant and wave kicked in. There has yet to be time to identify what was lost as we continue to have losses. There is no time to grieve the past as that past changes and morphs daily. It has been challenging to plan the future as we live in the unpredictable.

VUCA is a term coined by the US army to describe the Iraq and Afghanistan wars situation. VUCA is an acronym for volatile, uncertain, complex, and ambiguous. Change is rapid. There are no standard solutions or defined processes.

What does it take for organizations to survive and thrive in a VUCA world? First, it creates psychological safety for work teams, to utilize their collective intelligence to keep ahead of the rapid change.

Mindfulness for Teams

Personal Relationships: With work structured around the power of teams, it's essential for workers to feel involved and included to facilitate contribution. Having the space to openly bring viewpoints without hesitation, encourage healthy discussion, and feel connected with team members (even at a personal level), fosters a greater sense of belonging. To enhance personal relationships:

Find meaningful and inclusive ways to engage your colleagues that feel marginalized or excluded. Demonstrate trust and respect for your colleagues by leading with vulnerability, seeking clarity, checking assumptions, and avoiding defensiveness.

Show that you value and care for your colleagues by taking an interest in their stories and well-being. Practice behaviours that promote connection (open-door, turned-on camera) while respecting various working styles and preferences.

Frequently celebrate colleagues' successes and offer dedicated support through challenges. Find opportunities to express daily gratitude to those you work with (thank you notes, meeting spotlights, etc.).

CHAPTER TEN

The Future Is Now!

"With a new day comes new strengths and thoughts."
– Eleanor Roosevelt

The world is constantly changing and evolving. Many events are making us feel polarized, less stable, and volatile. External events like climate change, political instability, the global pandemic, racial discrimination, etc., are causing a sense of frustration, fear, and disruptions. The Russian war on Ukraine, the cost of living and a looming recession indicates the new normal, where uncertainty and volatility are the rules of the day. There has been a seismic shift, and the world is unpredictable. While we live in a time of information overload, we are aware of the unfortunate reality of disinformation.

A leader must understand the limitations of a single piece of information and a range of perspectives. We now talk about the predictability of the unpredictable. In the world of employment, there was much talk around the great resignation that started with COVID-19; now, that discourse is quickly dissipating, giving way to a new phrase: "quiet quitting." Driven by many of the same factors as actual resignations, quiet quitting refers to employees opting out of tasks beyond one's assigned duties and becoming less psychologically invested in work. While quiet quitters continue to fulfil their primary responsibilities, they are less willing to engage in work that goes above and beyond expectations. The issue sounds minor, but as a leader, you understand most jobs cannot be fully defined in a formal job description or contract. Organizations rely on employees' engagement to willingly step up and take on emerging work. Now, most leaders have asked which is better to deal with: resigning and leaving the organization or having people stay who only do the minimum job requirements? This is a question for reflection for you as a leader. I, for one, would like to lead a fully engaged team. A business thrives when employees use their discretionary effort to go above and beyond.

New buzzwords have come into the global vocabulary: great resignation, hybrid/remote work, digital fluency, and quiet quitting, all to show the daily speed of change. Scientists have taught us that our brains have neuroplasticity, which means our brains can continue to learn and grow. We have heard that knowledge is power, and recently I am hearing that learning is the superpower. In a world where the speed of change is almost outpacing us, the ability to unlearn and learn new skills and develop new habits is one of the critical traits of successful leaders post-COVID-19. Apple CEO Cook said, "Technology is a great thing that will accomplish many things, but unless you have diverse views at the table that are working on it, you don't wind up with great solutions." Belonging is good for business if workers feel like they belong; companies reap substantial bottom-line benefits. A high sense of belonging is linked to a 56% increase in job performance, a 50% drop in turnover risk and a 75% reduction in sick days.

There has been trepidation about people moving from offices and working from their homes. The anxiety was from both ends, from employees who had no space in their homes to make an office-like environment, to people who did not have good internet bandwidth, either because they could not afford it or because there was no coverage in their area. Then there was also the dynamic of partners and spouses working from home, creating 2 different office spaces; and as if that were not enough, children who had to learn from home.

A lot was going on for people in 2020. We started with the adrenal rush; when COVID-19 first hit, there was great anxiety and fear, and hope that this would come and go. Then as the year progressed, when countries moved from complete shutdown to levels of starting to come back, there was great anticipation of coming back to life in September 2021. However, the virus was not done and is here to stay, so we know better now than then. Countries entered the second wave, then the third wave and now. 2022 provided hope that life was coming back, with the vaccine rolled out and COVID-19 cases going down. Indeed, the doors opened, and new challenges came: the Russian war on Ukraine, inflation, labour shortages and a looming recession—never a dull moment on this planet—all to show that unless we build our agility and resilience, we will see more mental health issues, moral distress, burnout, resignation, and labour shortages. Some organizations have come full circle to realize that the focus is more than just on talent acquisition in this acute labour shortage environment. The focus should be retention first and then recruitment. As a leader, you have the responsibility to retain the good talent you already have; this is your biggest challenge.

On the other hand, managers and leaders were going through other anxieties and fears. Organizations still needed to produce results. Now managers were faced with the challenge of delivering results in a different environment. The office was a space of empowerment and comfort for the managers. They believed they had better control of their teams and were confident they would drive the results they needed. Things changed. Exercising control over people through physical presence changed and reaching out to people via technology put the fear of God in some managers and leaders. There were physiological and psychological challenges to managers and leaders. We need to remember that managers and leaders are people, too, and are employees as well. Mental health issues came up for both employees and leaders.

As the NeuroLeadership Institute, in their SCARF model, explains, human behaviour is driven by social threat and reward in status, certainty, autonomy, relatedness and fairness. Threat signals can make us feel like we are out of control and that our social safety is in danger. When these social threats are handled, some leaders react to those feelings of threat with attempts to regain control through surveillance. Many leaders felt that their jobs had changed entirely and wondered how they were expected to perform in a role they were not hired to perform. They were not hired to manage and lead remote employees. Some have resisted the use of technology for a long time. Many of the baby boomers were just hanging on for their last 2, 3, and 5 years before retirement and could not be bothered to learn new skills. For them, the old way of doing things was working. Why fix it if it's not broken? Why spend time learning?

In neuroscience, besides the ground-breaking discovery of brain plasticity, they also discovered that social threats could send signals in the brain like a physical threat, flight or fight survival mode. Whether the threat is real or perceived, the reaction is the same; our brains seek safety wherever we find it. One of the critical skills to learn is the choice and ability to treat differences with empathy and kindness. As Jacinda Arden, prime minister of New Zealand put it in her Harvard convocation speech, "After all, there are some things in this life that make this world small and connected; let kindness be one of them." Kindness to self is the starting point.

To survive the pandemic, many leaders resorted to surveillance. Now you will need to unlearn this habit to become an effective leader.

There is a difference between checking in and checking on a person. Monitored employees are less productive because they sense that their autonomy is under threat, and their brain is triggered into flight or fight survival mode. When employees feel they are not trusted, their psychological safety is threatened. Once they do not feel safe, employees cannot bring their best selves, affecting their productivity. This is because employees will use some of their energy to manage their fear of being caught outside the box and will go into avoidance mode. They will need to be more engaged to use their discretional effort to go above and beyond what is expected. There is no room for creativity as they focus on doing only what they are told and are void of taking risks.

Surveillance does not allow for flexibility and removes the leader's ability to lead people from where they are—what the Ken Blanchard group calls situational leadership.

Leaders and managers must learn digital fluency.

Tailored training and learning paths for technology-based communication platforms is key to successful leadership. To maximize the benefits of remote work in the space of inclusion, there is data that shows that diverse teams outperform homogeneous teams. Data also shows that leaders need to know how to be inclusive to maximize the benefits of inclusion. Similarly, leaders need to understand that employees working remotely can feel safer than onsite; they think their quality of life is improved by, for example, reducing the stress related to commuting and wasting time between places.

Design work around people by fostering a psychologically safe environment. The intentional balancing act between individual preferences and organizational needs is a balancing act in how we treat those who work from home versus those who work at the office.

Leaders should exercise empathy and act with compassion.

In recent years, much focus has been on empathy as part of effective leadership. Empathy is the ability to understand and share the feelings of another. Leaders should go beyond sensitivity to the feelings of the other, to acting. Empathy plus action leads to compassion. Empathy alone can look like the following scenario in the new world of working: An employee has an isolated child at home because there has been a

COVID-19 outbreak in their school. The leader can sympathize with the parent who can now not produce outputs during the day as she must help the child with homework. Acting is engaging the employee in co-creating the solution. Are there better working hours? Are some deadlines able to shift, and is there some urgent work that another team member can finish? Managers and leaders need to move from the traditional space of knowing it all, to learning it all and not having all the answers.

Make mental health mainstream.

Much has been shared and written about how most humans have had their mental health challenged by the pandemic, moving from the traditional space where mental health issues were scorned, to normalizing the need to be healthy. In my experience as a family lawyer or divorce attorney, as some call it, I have worked with parents going through separation and divorce. Many are so traumatized by the process that they lose their capacity to be fit to parent their children.

I learnt one fundamental aspect: Unless we are healthy as parents or leaders, we cannot parent or lead. Self-care cannot be over-emphasized. It is as if we had forgotten in our busyness that managers and leaders are humans too; they are employees too. Gone are the days when leaders are supposed to be superhuman, because such humans do not exist. As a leader, you need to know what matters to you and keep that front and centre of your work and personal life. Identify what your values and motivators are. Equally important is to identify what your limitations are. Guarding your mental health humanizes you and makes you relatable as a leader. Sharing your struggles and successes builds trust with your team. I know some leaders have reservations about being vulnerable and communicating with people reporting to them. I am not asking you to be an open book if that is not your style. I am suggesting that sharing relevant information that humanizes you is courage. You cannot be courageous without being vulnerable. You cannot inspire or influence if you are not relatable.

The world is complex now and is getting more complicated by the day. Future readiness means the ability to embrace an open growth mindset, and the openness to accept the reality that we have inter-cultural, inter-generational and inter-sectional ties, diversified aspects, and digital innovation. People are only accepting legacies of the past after questioning them. Right now, everyone is going through a transformation. The world has changed, and it will not go back to January 2020, when the world was open, and the pandemic was just starting. COVID-19 showed us that we are flexible humans, and now we need to flex our minds. We must embrace a growth mindset that opens us to opportunities to create a more inclusive and accepting world. A growth mindset seeks diversity of mind, is willing to be imperfect, leans into curiosity and away from judgment and strives for progress, not perfection.

In their ground-breaking collaboration joint study, Billie Jean King Leadership Initiative and Deloitte examined generational views of diversity and inclusion and their impact on innovation, engagement, and creativity. They found that millennials view inclusion as having a culture of connectors that facilitates teaming, collaboration, and professional growth. This view from the millennials starkly contrasts with prior generations who traditionally consider it from the perspective of representation and assimilation. What I found resonating is that millennials are much more concerned with cognitive diversity, or diversity of thoughts, ideas, and philosophies, and solving business problems through a culture of collaboration. Diversity of ideas and thinking and inviting everyone to share ideas, big or small, promotes innovation and provides a business advantage.

To be future proof, we must develop the change muscles now. We need to be digitally savvy, culturally intelligent, and agile. Leaders now require new capabilities to lead remote and distributed teams. If a leader is effective, employees are likely to be three times more engaged when they feel that the manager cares. Leaders are the catalyst for creating individual and team connections. Organizations are now to approach business from a human-centred design. Human-centred design is a seismic shift today and the future of work. Now more than ever, we see an accelerated effort and focus on the employee's well-being. For the first time, the employee's voice has become stronger than that of the organization. While demands on managers and leaders have always been high, the employee's voice has amplified, and expectations are high. New leadership models and capabilities are needed to cope with and thrive in this new environment of leading a remote/hybrid workforce.

In their article "The Radical Transformation of Diversity and Inclusion: The Millennial Influence," Deloitte University says millennials view inclusion as having a culture of connectedness that facilitates teaming, collaboration, and professional growth. Millennials are much more concerned with the diversity of thought, ideas and philosophies and solving problems collaboratively. By 2025, millennials will make up over 75% of the workforce. A business that does not adapt to new ways of inclusion will suffer from an inability to retain millennials and Generation Z (1996–2012). Gone are the days when looking at diversity through the lens of compliance or representation of gender, race, religion, ethnicity, and sexual orientation. Diversity is about unique experiences, identities, ideas, and opinions. Innovative companies like Apple and others are ahead in understanding that diversity is a variety of cultures and perspectives working together to solve business problems. Leaders must acknowledge that they must prepare the next generation to take over, by being supportive of individual perspectives.

Businesses that create connectional intelligence are the ones that will survive. Connectional intelligence combines cognitively diverse people, disciplines, and networks to create value, meaning and breakthroughs. This is achievable through openness to diverse perspectives. To be fully engaged, millennials require supportive leaders who promote a collaborative environment in which employees can see the impact of their work, understand the value they bring and recognize their efforts. I have been amazed by how millennials are quick to solve problems.

Inclusive leaders work on breaking down formal, inflexible hierarchies, adopting a bottom approach to ideation and problem-solving. Embracing social collaboration and allowing new ways of doing things go a long way in retaining talent. Leaders should know by now that our world is changing rapidly. Inclusion says come as you are. You fit right in. Assimilation says to become as I am to be considered a good fit. The factors that bring diverse talent into organizations are different from retaining talent. It is time to break down the old way of promoting diversity; do not put new wine into old wineskins.

In their book, *Hello Stay Interviews, Goodbye Talent Loss: A Manager's Playbook*, Beverly Kaye and Sharon Jordan-Evans share this cautionary message: "If you're not yet holding stay interviews, you are guessing at what your talented people really want—from you, from the team, from their work. You could be guessing wrong. Stay interviews are just one of many strategies in a successful manager's playbook. But they are foundational to engaging, motivating, recognizing, and retaining talent." Traditionally, companies would hold exit interviews. Considering the war for talent and the labour shortage we are experiencing; it is a futile exercise to conduct hundreds of exit interviews instead of stay interviews. The old formula was recruitment, then retention, but now companies have changed, and they focus more on retention first than recruitment. Research has shown that billions are lost yearly on losing talent.

As I conclude this book, I want to share a quote that has kept me motivated to pursue the work in Diversity, Equity, Inclusion and Belonging. Mahatma Gandhi said; "Our ability to reach unity in diversity will be the beauty and the test of our civilization."

ABOUT THE AUTHOR

Cecilia Ntombizodwa Mzvondiwa, BA. LLB. MA.

Cecilia was born and raised in Zimbabwe (Rhodesia). She attended the University of Zimbabwe and obtained a Bachelor of Arts with Dual Honors in Philosophy and Religion in 2000. Cecilia taught History and Religion at the Dominican Convent high school. She then moved to Canada at the end of 2001. In Canada, she pursued her education and obtained a master's degree in Human Security and Peace Building from Royal Roads University in Victoria, BC. She then enrolled in law school and received a Bachelor of Laws degree from the University of South Africa in 2014. She then worked on the conversion process to obtain her Canadian law degree equivalency through the Federal Law Societies of Canada, and then did her articles to practice law in Canada. To access legal advice, email her directly at cecilia@onpointlaw446.onmicrosoft.com.

She is highly versatile and currently serves her clients in multiple capacities. Primarily as a barrister and solicitor, she practices family law in Alberta, Canada, and immigration law for clients around the globe. A member of the John Maxwell team, she is a coach, a sought-after conference speaker and trainer, and a diversity and inclusion expert. As a seasoned diversity and inclusion expert, she is the founder and CEO of Global People First, a consultancy that focuses on diversity, equity and inclusion, and has a presence in North America, Europe, New Zealand and Australia. Her experiences with diverse clients propelled her to embark on this project, and her dream is to create a better corporate world where, irrespective of race or gender, our inalienable rights of life, liberty and the pursuit of happiness will be respected for all, and working together is how we achieve this goal. To book your free 30-minute discovery session on DEI services, email cecilia@globalpeoplefirst.com.

A Life-Long Learner

Cecilia is a life-long learner. She has worked as a human resource professional with Alberta Health Services. During that time, she also obtained the following certifications:

- A certified training and development professional
- A certified speaker, coach, and trainer
- A certified Canadian immigration consultant
- A leadership and change management professional

Community Involvement

Cecilia has lived in Grande Prairie since 2006. She has been actively involved in the local and international community in different ways.

She is a member of the Chamber of Commerce.

She is a current board member of the Community Foundations of Northwest Alberta.

She is currently a board member of the Grande Prairie Local Immigration Partnership.

She has been sought out as a keynote speaker for different organizations, locally and internationally.

Personal Interests

At home, Cecilia enjoys spending time with her daughter Mia.

She enjoys reading and blogging about personal development, diversity and inclusion, cultures and languages.

She travels the world to enjoy the beauty of our planet Earth.

She loves Zumba as she enjoys music and dance, and she also loves the outdoors.

You can learn more about the author by linking to her social media handles below:

https://www.instagram.com/globalpeoplefirst/
https://www.linkedin.com/in/cecilia-mzvondiwa-0a66b167/
https://www.facebook.com/zoe.mu

Beyond Tokenism is Cecilia's pursuit of a more accepting and inclusive world, a planet where humans can achieve the highest form of civilization by recognizing the fundamental rights of all humans. The book is based on science and research confirmed by human lived experiences. Her goal is to tell stories that show the business and human imperative for creating success through inclusion. To learn more about the book and leave a comment, you can go to the book website by clicking the link below.

www.ingramcontent.com/pod-product-compliance
Lightning Source LLC
Chambersburg PA
CBHW062045270326
41930CB00031B/2346